American Book Company's

MASTERING THE

GEORGIA 6TH GRADE

CRCT

IN

READING

Kristie White
Project Coordinator: Zuzana Urbanek
Executive Editor: Dr. Frank Pintozzi

American Book Company
PO Box 2638
Woodstock, GA 30188-1383
Toll Free: 1 (888) 264-5877   Phone: (770) 928-2834
Toll Free Fax: 1 (866) 827-3240
Web site: www.americanbookcompany.com

ACKNOWLEDGEMENTS

The authors wish to thank Lisa Cocca for her writing contribution. In addition, the authors would like to gratefully acknowledge the editing and technical contributions of Marsha Torrens and Yvonne Benson.

We also want to thank Charisse Johnson and Rachae Brooks for their expertise in developing the graphics for this book.

Preface   **v**

Test-Taking Tips vi

Diagnostic Test   **1**

Evaluation Chart for Diagnostic Test... 18

Chapter 1 Author's Purpose   **19**

Author's Purpose... 19
    Literature That Entertains.. 20
    Literature That Informs 21
    Literature That Expresses 22
    Literature That Persuades 22
Context for Reading 24
Chapter 1 Summary... 25
Chapter 1 Review.. 26

Chapter 2   Paragraph Structure and Main Idea   **31**

Paragraphs.. 31
Main Idea 32
Topic Sentence 32
Supporting Ideas and Details 33
Concluding Sentences 33
Recognizing Hidden Main Ideas in Informational Texts...................... 34
Chapter 2 Summary... 37
Chapter 2 Review.. 38

Chapter 3   Structure and Patterns in Writing   **41**

Transitions.. 41
Sequence of Events 41
Cause and Effect 44
Classification Schemes and Logical Order 45
Definition 45
Comparison and Contrast 45
Chapter 3 Summary... 48
Chapter 3 Review.. 49

Chapter 4   Reading Persuasive Nonfiction and Multistep Instructions 53

Propaganda Techniques 53
    Card Stacking 54
    Bandwagon 54
    Testimonial 55
    Glittering Generalities 55
    Repetition 56
    Transfer 56
Understanding Multistep Instructions 57
Chapter 4 Summary 59
Chapter 4 Review 60

Chapter 5   Graphics and Organization in Informational Texts   63

Common Features of Informational Texts 63
Glossaries 64
Indices 64
Graphics 65
    Graphic Organizers 65
    Illustrations and Captions 66
        Activity 1: Graphics 67
    Diagrams and Graphs 68
        Activity 2: More Graphics 69
    Charts and Tables 70
Evaluating the Merits of Text 70
Chapter 5 Summary 73
Chapter 5 Review 74

Chapter 6   Sensory Details and Figurative Language   79

Figurative Language 79
Idioms 80
Metaphor 82
Simile 83
Hyperbole 85
Personification 86
Alliteration 88
Onomatopoeia 89
Chapter 6 Summary 90
Chapter 6 Review 91

Chapter 7   Basic Elements of Story Structure   95

Setting 95
Characterization 97
Protagonist and Antagonist 99
Conflict 100
    Man vs. Self 100
    Man vs. Man 101
    Man vs. Nature 101
    Man vs. Society 101
Plot 102

Introduction..102
Rising Action..103
Climax..103
Falling Action...103
Resolution...103
Chapter 7 Summary...105
Chapter 7 Review..106

Chapter 8   Advanced Elements of Story Structure   111

Dialogue 111
Description 114
Historical Setting...115
Speaker and Point of View...............................117
Theme and Message 119
   Theme 119
   Message 120
Chapter 8 Summary...123
Chapter 8 Review..124

Chapter 9   Reading and Understanding Literature and Poetry   129

Tone...129
Sound..131
Alliteration 131
Onomatopoeia..133
Rhyme Scheme 134
Graphics 135
Chapter 9 Summary...137
Chapter 9 Review..138

Chapter 10 Vocabulary   141

Context Clues..142
Synonyms and Antonyms.................................144
Word Meaning across Subjects.........................144
Words with Multiple Meanings 145
Greek and Latin Roots and Affixes..................146
   Commonly Used Greek and Latin Roots and Affixes.........................147
Vocabulary in Various Subjects........................149
Chapter 10 Summary.......................................150
Chapter 10 Review..151

Practice Test 1   155
Practice Test 2   171
Index   187

PREFACE

Mastering the Georgia 6th Grade CRCT in Reading will help students who are learning or reviewing material for the CRCT. The materials in this book are based on the GPS standards as published by the Georgia Department of Education.

This book contains several sections. These sections are as follows: 1) general information about the book; 2) a diagnostic test; 3) an evaluation chart; 4) chapters that teach the concepts and skills that improve CRCT readiness; 5) two practice tests. Answers to the tests and exercises are in a separate manual. The answer manual also contains a chart of standards for teachers to make a more precise diagnosis of student needs and assignments and a section of activities for extension and differentiation.

We welcome comments and suggestions about the book. Please contact us at

American Book Company
PO Box 2638
Woodstock, GA 30188-1383

Toll Free: 1 (888) 264-5877
Phone: (770) 928-2834
Fax: (770) 928-7483
Web site: www.americanbookcompany.com

ABOUT THE AUTHOR

Kristie White is a language arts teacher in the Georgia Public School System. Since 2000, she has taught a variety of language arts and English courses ranging from the middle grades through the college level. Her Ed.S. degree is from Mercer University.

About the Project Coordinator: Zuzana Urbanek serves as ELA Curriculum Coordinator for American Book Company. She is a professional writer with 25 years of experience in education, business, and publishing. She has taught a variety of English courses since 1990 at the college level and also taught English as a foreign language abroad. Her master's degree is from Arizona State University.

About the Executive Editor: Dr. Frank J. Pintozzi is a former Professor of Education at Kennesaw (GA) State University. For over 28 years, he has taught English and reading at the high school and college levels as well as in teacher preparation courses in language arts and social studies. In addition to writing and editing state standard-specific texts for high school exit and end of course exams, he has edited and written numerous college textbooks.

TEST-TAKING TIPS

1. Complete the chapters and practice tests in this book. This text will help you review the skills for the CRCT in Reading.

2. Be prepared. Get a good night's sleep the day before your exam. Eat a well-balanced meal, one that contains plenty of proteins and carbohydrates, prior to your exam.

3. Arrive early. Allow yourself at least 15–20 minutes to find your room and get settled. Then you can relax before the exam, so you won't feel rushed.

4. Think success. Keep your thoughts positive. Turn negative thoughts into positive ones. Tell yourself you will do well on the exam.

5. Practice relaxation techniques. Some students become overly worried about exams. Before or during the test, they may perspire heavily, experience an upset stomach, or have shortness of breath. If you feel any of these symptoms, talk to a close friend or see a counselor. They will suggest ways to deal with test anxiety. Here are some quick ways to relieve test anxiety:

   • Imagine yourself in your most favorite place. Let yourself sit there and relax.

   • Do a body scan. Tense and relax each part of your body starting with your toes and ending with your forehead.

   • Use the 3-12-6 method of relaxation when you feel stress. Inhale slowly for 3 seconds. Hold your breath for 12 seconds, and then exhale slowly for 6 seconds.

6. Read directions carefully. If you don't understand them, ask the proctor for further explanation before the exam starts.

7. Use your best approach for answering the questions. Some test-takers like to skim the questions and answers before reading the problem or passage. Others prefer to work the problem or read the passage before looking at the answers. Decide which approach works best for you.

8. Answer each question on the exam. Unless you are instructed not to, make sure you answer every question. If you are not sure of an answer, take an educated guess. Eliminate choices that are definitely wrong, and then choose from the remaining answers.

9. Use your answer sheet correctly. Make sure the number on your question matches the number on your answer sheet. In this way, you will record your answers correctly. If you need to change your answer, erase it completely. Smudges or stray marks may affect the grading of your exams, particularly if they are scored by a computer. If your answers are on a computerized grading sheet, make sure the answers are dark. The computerized scanner may skip over answers that are too light.

10. Check your answers. Review your exam to make sure you have chosen the best responses. Change answers only if you are sure they are wrong.

GA 6th Grade CRCT Reading Diagnostic Test

The purpose of this diagnostic test is to measure your knowledge in reading comprehension. This diagnostic test is based on the GPS-based CRCT standards for Reading and adheres to the sample question format provided by the Georgia Department of Education.

General Directions:

1. Read all directions carefully.

2. Read each question or sample. Then choose the best answer.

3. Choose only one answer for each question. If you change an answer, be sure to erase your original answer completely.

4. After taking the test, you or your instructor should score it using the evaluation chart following the test. This will enable you to determine your strengths and weaknesses. Then study chapters in this book corresponding to topics that you need to review.

The Man, the Boy, and the Donkey

by Aesop

A Man and his son were once going with their Donkey to market. As they were walking along by its side, a countryman passed them and said: "You fools, what is a Donkey for, but to ride upon?"

So the Man put the Boy on the Donkey, and they went on their way. But soon they passed a group of men, one of whom said: "See that lazy youngster; he lets his father walk while he rides."

So the Man ordered his Boy to get off, and got on himself. But they hadn't gone far when they passed two women, one of whom said to the other: "Shame on that lazy lout to let his poor little son trudge along."

Well, the Man didn't know what to do, but at last he took his Boy up before him on the Donkey. By this time they had come to the town, and the passers-by began to jeer and point at them. The Man stopped and asked what they were scoffing at. The men said: "Aren't you ashamed of yourself for overloading that poor Donkey of yours—you and your hulking son?"

The Man and Boy got off and tried to think what to do. They thought and they thought, till at last they cut down a pole, tied the Donkey's feet to it, and raised the pole and the Donkey to their shoulders. They went along amid the laughter of all who met them till they came to Market Bridge, when the Donkey, getting one of his feet loose, kicked out and caused the Boy to drop his end of the pole. In the struggle the Donkey fell over the bridge, and his fore-feet being tied together he was drowned.

---

1. What is the theme of the fable?   ELA6R1.d

   A. Do not judge by appearance alone.

   B. Try to please all and you will please none.

   C. A man's actions speak louder than his words.

   D. The wisest of men listens to the wisdom of others.

2. The story is told from the point of view of   ELA6R1.f

   A. the boy.   **C.** the donkey.

   B. the man.   **D.** the narrator.

3. The **main** conflict in the fable is **best** described as   ELA6R1.e

   A. man against boy.

   B. man against self.

   C. man against river.

   D. man against donkey.

4. In paragraph 4, the word *jeer* **most closely** means   ELA6R2.a

   A. ridicule.   **C.** accompany.

   B. applaud.   **D.** photograph.

5. The author uses dialogue in the story to help the reader   ELA6R1.b

   A. picture the setting.

   B. feel sorry for the Donkey.

   C. understand the conflict.

   D. see the boy's point of view.

2

Chester Used His Head

(1) A great idea can come from a simple need. Chester Greenwood learned that lesson at a young age. He grew up in Maine where the winter air is often freezing cold. People bundled up and braved the icy cold weather every day. The young people in town wrapped a woolen scarf around their heads and went outside. They hurried to complete their chores, so they could enjoy some time on the frozen pond.

(2) Chester liked to have fun just like every other fifteen-year-old in town. One especially cold day in 1873, he picked up his new ice skates and headed for the pond. He laced up his skates and raced across the ice. The wind cut through the trees like a knife and pushed across the glassy surface. The skaters wrapped their scarves tighter around their heads. Unfortunately for Chester, this solution did not work for him. The woolen scarves caused an itchy rash to appear on his skin. Chester tried to keep up with the other boys on the ice, but his ears turned bright red and ached. Before long, he had to remove his skates and go home.

(3) Chester was unhappy with his choices. He needed to discover a way to stay outside in the cold with his friends and be comfortable. He needed to find a simple solution to his problem. At home, Chester took a piece of wire and bent the ends into two loops. Next, he asked his grandmother to sew fur and fabric onto the loops. When she was done, Chester placed his invention on his ears. He had invented the first pair of earmuffs.

(4) Wearing earmuffs, Chester could skate all afternoon. At first his friends teased him about his furry ears. Chester didn't let that discourage him. He kept wearing his invention and telling his friends how warm his ears felt. Before long, Chester's friends were asking him to make ear protectors for them.

(5) Chester was nineteen when he received a patent for his invention. The document said that only Chester could make his earmuffs. He opened a factory and started making and selling his ear protectors.

(6) Chester kept improving his invention. He found a way to make his ear protectors so they could fold up and fit in a pocket. This made them much more portable. He also made the earmuffs with different materials.

(7) Chester needed help getting earmuffs to everyone who needed them. He opened a factory and hired many workers. By the time he was twenty-eight years old, Chester's business was selling ear protectors around the world. He even sold earmuffs to the army during World War I. The ear protectors kept the soldiers' ears warm.

(8) Chester thought of many new ways to solve problems. He invented more than 100 different things. People in Maine still honor the inventor. Every December 21, they celebrate Chester Greenwood Day.

6. The article is **mainly** about   ELA6R1.d

   A. inventing the earmuff.

   B. dealing with allergies.

   C. the cold winter weather in Maine.

   D. celebrating Chester Greenwood Day.

7. The organization of the article can **best** be described as   ELA6R1.c

   A. time order.

   B. comparison.

   C. general to specific.

   D. order of importance.

8. The author's purpose in writing the article was **most likely** to

   ELA6RC2.e

   A. sell the reader earmuffs.

   B. help the reader picture Maine.

   C. explain how earmuffs were invented.

   D. teach readers the importance of a patent.

9. Which sentence would **best** support the topic sentence in paragraph 7?

   ELA6R1.d

   A. Earmuffs are only worn in areas with cold weather.

   B. Today, earmuffs come in every color of the rainbow.

   C. One year his workers made 400,000 pairs of earmuffs.

   D. Chester Greenwood is one of Maine's best known inventors.

10. The word *portable* comes from the Latin root word *port*. What is the definition of the word *portable* as it is used in paragraph 6?

    ELA6R2.b

    A. easy to bend

    B. easy to carry

    C. costly to buy

    D. warm to wear

11. A reader wants to learn about Chester's other ideas. Using an encyclopedia of inventors, what keyword in the index will **most** help the reader?

    ELA6R1.a

    A. Maine

    B. weather

    C. inventor

    D. Greenwood

"The Schoolboy" by William Blake

I love to rise in a summer morn,
When the birds sing on every tree;
The distant huntsman winds his horn,
And the skylark sings with me:
O what sweet company!   **(1)**

But to go to school in a summer morn, –
O it drives all joy away!
Under a cruel eye outworn,
The little ones spend the day
In sighing and dismay.   **(2)**

Ah then at times I drooping sit,
And spend many an anxious hour;
Nor in my book can I take delight,
Nor sit in learning's bower,
Worn through with the dreary shower.   **(3)**

How can the bird that is born for joy
Sit in a cage and sing?
How can a child, when fears annoy,
But droop his tender wing,
And forget his youthful spring!   **(4)**

O father and mother if buds are nipped,
And blossoms blown away;
And if the tender plants are stripped
Of their joy in the springing day,
By sorrow and care's dismay, –   **(5)**

How shall the summer arise in joy,
Or the summer fruits appear?
Or how shall we gather what griefs destroy,
Or bless the mellowing year,
When the blasts of winter appear?   **(6)**

12. In stanza 4, the bird is a metaphor for the

ELA6R1.a

    A. classroom.

    B. schoolboy.

    C. summer.

    D. skylark.

13. The influence of the Industrial Revolution on the poem can **best** be seen in

ELA6R1.c

    A. the setting of the poem.

    B. the rhythm of the poem.

    C. the shifting narrative point of view.

    D. the antagonist/protagonist relationship.

14. Why does the author use the words *cruel*, *dismay*, *dreary*, and *tender*?

ELA6R1.g

    A. to set the tone

    B. to describe the boy

    C. to identify the setting

    D. to create the rhyme pattern

15. What is the **main** conflict found in the poem?

ELA6R1.e

    A. boy versus self

    B. boy versus book

    C. boy versus nature

    D. boy versus authority

16. Which word **best** describes the schoolboy in the poem?

ELA6R1.e

    A. sad

    B. lonely

    C. curious

    D. excited

A Sweet Experiment

Have you ever grown candy? This sweet science experiment will show you how.

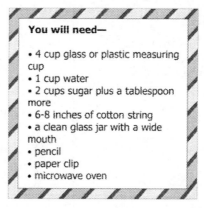

You will need—

• 4 cup glass or plastic measuring cup
• 1 cup water
• 2 cups sugar plus a tablespoon more
• 6-8 inches of cotton string
• a clean glass jar with a wide mouth
• pencil
• paper clip
• microwave oven

Safety First!

(1) The first rule of all science experiments is safety. You will use boiling water to grow your rock candy. **Work carefully under the supervision of an adult.**

Let's Get Started

(2) After gathering your materials, tie one end of the string to the pencil and the other end to the paper clip. Next, pour one cup of water into the measuring cup. Then, add one cup of the sugar to the water and stir. After the sugar dissolves in the water, place the measuring cup in a microwave oven. Heat the sugar water solution on high for two minutes. Carefully take the measuring cup out of the oven. The liquid will be very hot.

(3) Stir the sugar water again. Add a second cup of sugar to the solution and stir some more. Be careful not to spill or splash the liquid. Put the cup back into the oven and heat it for an additional two minutes. Remove the hot liquid from the oven and stir until all of the sugar dissolves in the water. Put the liquid back in the microwave oven one last time. Heat it for one minute and remove the sugar water from the oven.

(4) Lay the pencil across the mouth of the jar. Drop the paper clip into the jar. It will work like an anchor holding the string in place. Wind the string around the pencil so the string hangs straight without touching the bottom of the jar. Remove the pencil and string from the jar without unwinding the string. Slowly, pour the hot liquid into the jar.

(5) Dampen the string with cool water and roll it in the extra tablespoon of sugar. Lay the pencil across the mouth of the jar again and drop the paper clip anchor into the liquid.

Be Patient!

(6) Wait a couple of hours before making your first observation. Then, look for crystals forming on the string. Let the rock candy crystals grow for about a week before removing them from the jar. The solution cannot be used again. Discard the remaining liquid and wash the jar with soapy water. Break off a piece of your rock candy and enjoy your sweet science experiment!

17. Which group would find the article **most** helpful? ELA6RC2.d

    A. candy store clerks

    B. sugar cane growers

    C. students planning a science fair

    D. manufacturers of microwave ovens

18. What is the **main** message of the article? ELA6RC2.a

    A. Life is sweet.

    B. Science is fun.

    C. Any place can be a science lab.

    D. Safety should be your first concern.

19. What **most likely** is the author's purpose in placing some information in a box? ELA6RC2.f

    A. to make it easier for the reader to gather materials

    B. to show that the information isn't a main part of the article

    C. to suggest that other experiments can be completed with the same materials

    D. to warn readers that the experiment requires many materials not found at home

20. What should you do to the string before rolling it in the sugar? ELA6R1.e

    A. Dip it in the sugar water.

    B. Dampen it with cool water.

    C. Unwind the string from the pencil.

    D. Remove the paper clip from the string.

21. Why do the directions include stirring the liquid many times? ELA6R1.d

    A. to cool the water between steps

    B. to remind people to work safely

    C. to allow many people to participate

    D. to keep the sugar dissolved in the water

22. Which sentence uses the word *solution* in the same way it is used in the article? ELA6RC3.a

    A. The detective always gathers his clues before arriving at the correct solution.

    B. The teacher wants to see the work as well as the solution to the math problem.

    C. My mother uses a solution of lemon juice and vinegar to clean the kitchen sink.

    D. I had almost given up finding the solution to my problem when I found the answer.

23. After reading, a student wants to determine the meaning of the word *anchor* as it is used in the article. What strategy would **best** help the student? ELA6RC4.c

    A. reread paragraph 4

    B. read the topic sentences

    C. study the title and headings

    D. scan the list of needed materials

I bought Tri-Spot Socks for my whole family. Wearing the socks has turned exercise into a fun part of our family routine. We no longer spend our "down time" sitting in front of a television. Instead, we participate in weekly bike rides in the park and hikes on the mountain. On school nights, we enjoy a hopscotch tournament or a game of basketball. And because Tri-Spot Socks have kept us from being benched with sore feet, I know this new routine will become a permanent routine.

– Dr. Sophie Smith, podiatrist and mother of six

•••Tri-Spot

Before Tri-Spot Socks

After Tri-Spot Socks

Get Up! Get Together! Get Moving!

Today, families understand the importance of exercising together. Parents know the best way to get their children moving is to join in the fun with them. Whether families choose to jog, skip rope, or play hopscotch, their feet take a beating. What can parents do to make sure their children remain both active and healthy? Everyone knows to start with a sturdy, supportive sneaker. Many families have found though that even buying the best shoe available does not stop the formation of painful blisters. Loving, concerned parents are solving this problem with a pair of Tri-Spot Socks.

Tri-Spot Socks offer extra thick cushioning where your feet need it most – at the heel, toes, and the ball of your foot. Available in sizes for men, women, and children, Tri-Spot Socks take the worrying out of exercising as a family. With a pair of Tri-Spot Socks on each member of the family, moms and dads can feel secure in knowing their children will get the exercise they need without compromising their comfort or health.

Before Wearing Tri-Spot Socks	After Wearing Tri-Spot Socks
Children exercised 15 minutes per day	Children exercised 60 minutes per day
Children earned C+ grades in school	Children earned B+ grades in school

24. What **most likely** is the author's purpose for writing the Web page?   ELA6RC2.e

   A. to explain the benefits of daily exercise

   B. to persuade people to buy Tri-Spot Socks

   C. to inform readers about the variety of ways to exercise

   D. to describe the different kinds of injuries related to sports

25. Which sentence from the Web page contains loaded words?   ELA6LSV2.a

   A. I bought Tri-Spot Socks for my whole family.

   B. Everyone knows to start with a sturdy, supportive sneaker.

   C. Loving, concerned parents are solving this problem with a pair of Tri-Spot Socks.

   D. Instead, we participate in weekly bike rides in the park and hikes on the mountain.

26. The information in the box on the left is a propaganda technique known as ELA6LSV2.a

    A. testimonial.

    B. bandwagon.

    C. transfer.

    D. vague words.

27. The author uses the chart to ELA6LSV2.a

    A. show socks are available in children's sizes.

    B. explain that not all families own the socks yet.

    C. illustrate the need for three points of cushioning on the foot.

    D. suggest that the socks will help students perform better in school.

28. The author tries to persuade the reader with ELA6LSV2.a

    A. clear promises.

    B. scientific data.

    C. a friendly tone.

    D. basic statistics.

29. What is the purpose of the before-and-after illustrations? ELA6LSV2.a

    A. to persuade readers families are happier wearing the socks

    B. to illustrate the need for hiking as a regular part of exercise

    C. to help the reader picture themselves exercising regularly

    D. to explain how the Tri-Spot socks were originally made

30. What is the meaning of the word *benched* in the Web page? ELA6RC3.a

    A. playing sports

    B. running races

    C. watching television

    D. stopping exercise

Adapted from "A Handful of Clay"
by Henry Van Dyke

There was a handful of clay in the bank of a river. It was only common clay, coarse and heavy; but it had high thoughts of its own value, and wonderful dreams of the great place which it was to fill in the world when the time came for its virtues to be discovered.

(2) Waiting in its bed, the clay comforted itself with lofty hopes. "My time will come," it said. "I was not made to be hidden forever. Glory and beauty and honor are coming to me in due season."

One day the clay felt itself taken from the place where it had waited so long. A flat blade of iron passed beneath it, and lifted it, and tossed it into a cart with other lumps of clay. It was carried far away over a rough and stony road. But it was not afraid or discouraged, for it said to itself: "This is necessary. The path to glory is always rugged. Now I am on my way to play a great part in the world."

(4) But the hard journey was nothing compared with the distress that came after it. The clay was put into a trough and mixed and beaten and stirred and trampled. It seemed almost unbearable. But there was consolation in the thought that something very fine and noble was certainly coming out of all this trouble. The clay felt sure that, if it could only wait long enough, a wonderful reward was in store for it.

Then it was put upon a swiftly turning wheel, and whirled around until it seemed as if it must fly into a thousand pieces. A strange power pressed it and molded it, as it revolved, and through all the dizziness and pain it felt that it was taking a new form.

(6) Then an unknown hand put it into an oven, and fires were kindled about it—fierce and penetrating—hotter than all the heats of summer that had ever brooded upon the bank of the river. But through all, the clay held itself together and endured its trials, in the confidence of a great future. "Surely," it thought, "I am intended for something very splendid, since such pains are taken with me. Perhaps I am fashioned for the ornament of a temple, or a precious vase for the table of a king."

At last the baking was finished. The clay was taken from the furnace and set down upon a board, in the cool air, under the blue sky. The reward was at hand.

(8) Close beside the board there was a pool of water calm enough to reflect every image that fell upon it. There, for the first time, as it was lifted from the board, the clay saw its new shape, the reward of all its patience and pain—a common flower-pot, straight and stiff, red and ugly. And then it felt that it was not destined for a king's house, because it was made without glory or beauty or honor; and it murmured against the unknown maker, saying, "Why hast thou made me thus?"

Many days it passed in sullen discontent. Then it was filled with earth, and something—it knew not what—but something rough and brown and dead-looking, was thrust into the middle of the earth and covered over. The clay rebelled at this new disgrace. "This is the worst of all that has happened to me, to be filled with dirt and rubbish. Surely I am a failure."

(10) It was set in a greenhouse where the sunlight fell warm upon it and water was sprinkled over it. Day by day, as it waited, a change began to come to it. Something was stirring within it—a new hope. Still it was ignorant, not knowing what the new hope meant.

One day the clay was lifted again from its place, and carried into a great church. Its dream was coming true after all. It had a fine part to play in the world. Glorious music flowed over it. It was surrounded with flowers. Still it could not understand. So it whispered to another vessel of clay, like itself, close beside it, "Why have they set me here? Why do all the people look toward us?" And the other vessel answered, "Do you not know? You are carrying regal lilies. Their petals are white as snow, and the heart of them is like pure gold. The people look this way because the flower is the most wonderful in the world. And the root of it is in your heart."

(12) Then the clay was content, and silently thanked its maker, because, though an earthen vessel, it held so great a treasure.

31. The clay's ability to speak and dream is an example of   ELA6R1.a

   A. hyperbole.

   B. alliteration.

   C. onomatopoeia.

   D. personification.

32. What is the **main** theme of the story?   ELA6R1.d

   A. Slow but steady wins the race.

   B. Follow the path least traveled.

   C. Don't judge a book by its cover.

   D. Think twice before speaking once.

33. Throughout the story, the clay can be **best** described as   ELA6R1.e

   A. vain.

   B. happy.

   C. excited.

   D. curious.

34. The clay was not discouraged by the trip from the river to the furnace because   ELA6R1.e

   A. it was an easy trip.

   B. he was with other clays.

   C. it was exactly what he was expecting.

   D. he believed good would come from it.

35. The author uses dialogue to show the reader   ELA6R1.b

   A. the story is set long ago.

   B. the organization of the story.

   C. the basic steps of pottery making.

   D. the importance of all living things.

36. As it is used in paragraph 1, the word *bank* means   ELA6R2.c

   A. a set or row of elevators.

   B. the sideways turn of an airplane.

   C. the rising ground around a body of water.

   D. a place where money is held or exchanged.

When Is a Star Not a Star?

Have you ever wished upon a falling or shooting star? You might be surprised to learn that a falling or shooting star is not a star at all. The streaks of light that cut across the night sky are actually **meteoroids**. Made up of tiny bits of dust and grit, meteoroids burn up as they enter the earth's **atmosphere**. The result is a brief, bright trail of light in the sky.

If you have never seen a shooting star, you may also be surprised to learn that millions of shooting stars form every day. Although the short-lived streaks form at all times of the day, there are prime times for viewing them. Stargazers are about twice as likely to find a shooting or falling star in the few hours before dawn. At that time, the moon is low in the night sky. From that position, the moon shines much less light across the sky. The result is a dark canvas on which the burning meteoroids can be seen.

Meteor showers occur at certain times of year. On a typical night, you can spot a shooting star every fifteen minutes or so. During a meteor shower, you can see shooting stars every few minutes. A meteor shower occurs when the earth passes through the trail of debris left behind by **comets** that **orbit** the sun.

Occasionally, a piece of rock survives the fiery trip and lands on Earth. Scientists call this meteoroid remnant a **meteorite**. They study the meteorites to learn more about our **solar system**.

Glossary

Atmosphere – layer of gases surrounding the surface of a planet, moon, or star

Comet – a ball or rock and ice that orbits the sun

Meteor – a brief, bright streak of light formed when a meteoroid enters the earth's atmosphere

Meteorite – the remains of a meteoroid that falls to the earth's surface

Meteoroid – a small solid object moving through space

Meteor Shower – a large number of meteors that appear together in the same area of the sky

Orbit – to move in a circular path

Solar System – the Sun and its surrounding matter including comets, planets and moons

37. Why is it best to look for shooting stars a few hours before dawn?   ELA6R1.d

   A. There are few people around.

   B. The sky is darkest at that time.

   C. Air conditions are calmer then.

   D. The moon is brightest at dawn.

38. What is the purpose of the bold text in the article?   ELA6RC2.f

   A. to give synonyms for shooting stars

   B. to show emphasis for reading aloud

   C. to highlight words found in the glossary

   D. to show which paragraphs are important

Use the **glossary** to answer the next question.

39. Which statement is **most likely** true?   ELA6R1.a

    A. A chunk of the atmosphere landed in my yard.

    B. People sometimes call comets "dirty snowballs."

    C. I saw a collection of old meteors in the science museum.

    D. The meteorite didn't survive its flaming journey in the sky.

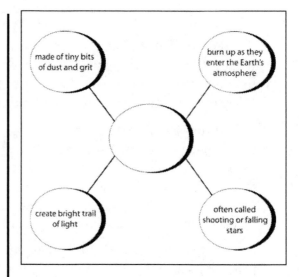

40. This article would be **most** helpful to   ELA6RC2.d

    A. pilots.

    B. scientists.

    C. rock collectors.

    D. new stargazers.

41. What was the author's **main** purpose in writing this article?   ELA6RC2.e

    A. to explain shooting stars

    B. to describe the night sky

    C. to sell meteor umbrellas

    D. to invite people outdoors

42. In the last paragraph, the word *remnant* means   ELA6RC3.a

    A. a flame.

    B. a season.

    C. a small surviving part.

    D. a planet orbiting the sun.

43. What **best** completes the graphic organizer?   ELA6R1.b

    A. stargazers

    B. meteoroids

    C. comet tails

    D. space science

The Bridge

(1) A rope bridge!" Michelle announced, as the girls approached an opening in the forest. "This is going to be fun!"

(2) Laura examined the bridge while she pondered the statement. If the builders had suspended the bridge over solid ground, it would be fun. Indeed, if it were over land, she would be racing her best friend across the wooden planks and enjoying the struggle to maintain her balance. But the bridge did not hang over dry ground; instead it wavered over fast flowing water. This was a whole different ballgame.

(3) Laura studied the water pushing past them in the river below. The raging waters slapped against the boulders jutting up from the riverbed. White foam formed beards on the faces of the rocks giving them a particularly menacing look. Laura shivered. The girls had first heard the river at least a mile back. Michelle had called it an invitation to adventure. In Laura's mind, the roar of the rushing river was more of a taunt. It was as if the river knew how she felt and was daring her to come closer.

(4) "Hurry!" Michelle shouted, as she clambered across the bridge.

(5) Laura shaded her eyes with her hand and squinted to see her friend run across the rippling bridge. Michelle reached the mid-point of the bridge, leaned on the rail of the swaying structure, and peered out into the distance. "Come on," Michelle yelled. "You have to see the view from here. It's absolutely spectacular!"

(6) Laura gripped the railing and inched her way onto the bridge. She heard the boards creak and felt them bow slightly. Although she was no more than an arm's length from her starting point, Laura knew she could advance no further. She stood as stiff as a statue staring down at the water swirling between the boulders. She felt certain that she was only moments away from having the rocking cradle that held her drop her into the whirlpool below. She shuddered as she considered the unknown creatures that lurked below the murky surface.

(7) "Hold onto me," Michelle whispered.

(8) Laura looked up. Michelle had forfeited her spot in the center of the bridge to return for her.

(9) "You'll be okay," Michelle said. "I'll help you across."

(10) Laura pried one hand off of the railing and grabbed hold of Michelle's arm. The girls began shuffling across the bridge. "Do you remember the first time we camped out?" Michelle asked.

(11) Laura nodded her head, and Michelle continued to speak. "We set up that little orange pup tent in your backyard. I thought it was so much fun until the sun dipped below the horizon. Once the sun disappeared, everything looked spooky through the tent wall. It was clear to me that our dim flashlights were no match for whatever lurked outside. I wanted to go home immediately and sleep in my own room far away from all of those creepy night noises. You, however, weren't afraid of anything and were determined to keep me there. You recognized every shadow and sound and helped me identify them too. That's the night you taught me the So Long Scary song. We sang that song numerous times until I finally fell asleep. By then I had memorized the words. Do you remember the words?"

(12) Laura sang, her voice shaking, as the girls slowly slid their feet across the rope and planks bridge. After making steady progress, they arrived at the other side. Laura glanced over her shoulder at the river and soaked in the feeling of deep satisfaction. She no longer felt burdened by her previous fears. In fact, Laura knew that now she could cross the bridge independently. With her friend's assistance, she had conquered her fear of her watery opponent.

44. In paragraph 6, the author uses "rocking cradle" as a metaphor for   ELA6R1.a

    A. the rocks.

    B. the bridge.

    C. Laura's fears.

    D. swirling waters.

45. What word describes both Laura and Michelle?   ELA6R1.e

    A. careless

    B. fearless

    C. defensive

    D. supportive

46. The **main** conflict of the story can **best** be described as   ELA6R1.e

    A. girl versus self.

    B. girl versus girl.

    C. girl versus society.

    D. girl versus technology.

47. The tone of the story can **best** be described as   ELA6R1.g

    A. sad.

    B. funny.

    C. mysterious.

    D. suspenseful.

48. How **most likely** would the story change if the bridge were **not** over a river?   ELA6R1.e

    A. The girls would get lost.

    B. The bridge would not sway.

    C. Laura would not feel afraid.

    D. Michelle would stay home.

49. Which situation below is **most** like the plot of the story, "The Bridge"?   ELA6RC4.a

    A. Jack is afraid of sleeping in the dark, so his mother buys him a nightlight.

    B. Lynn is afraid of snakes, until she finds a small snake in her own garden.

    C. Jim is afraid of climbing ladders, so his best friend goes into the attic for him.

    D. Sue and Tom help each other overcome their fear of performing in the school play.

50. The author uses "the roar of the rushing river" to help the reader   ELA6R1.h

    A. see and hear the river.

    B. identify the main character.

    C. see the importance of the bridge.

    D. think about the river as a person.

EVALUATION CHART FOR 6TH GRADE CRCT GEORGIA READING DIAGNOSTIC TEST

Directions: On the following chart, circle the question numbers that you answered incorrectly, and evaluate the results. These questions are based on the *Georgia Performance Standards (GPS) for 6th Grade Reading.* Then turn to the appropriate chapters, read the explanations, and complete the exercises. Review other chapters as needed. Finally, complete the practice test(s) to assess your progress and further prepare you for the **Georgia 6th Grade CRCT in Reading**.

Note: Some question numbers will appear under multiple chapters because those questions require demonstration of multiple skills.

Chapter	Diagnostic Test Question(s)
Chapter 1: Author's Purpose	8, 19, 24, 42, 49
Chapter 2: Paragraph Structure and Main Idea	6, 9, 11, 37, 40
Chapter 3: Structure and Patterns in Writing	7, 13
Chapter 4: Reading Persuasive Nonfiction and Multistep Instructions	20, 21, 25, 26, 27, 28, 29
Chapter 5: Graphics and Organization in Informational Texts	17, 38, 39, 41
Chapter 6: Sensory Details and Figurative Language	12, 31, 44, 50
Chapter 7: Basic Elements of Story Structure	3, 15, 16, 33, 34, 45, 46, 48
Chapter 8: Advanced Elements of Story Structure	1, 2, 5, 18, 32, 35
Chapter 9: Reading and Understanding Literature and Poetry	14, 47, 50
Chapter 10: Vocabulary	4, 10, 22, 23, 30, 36, 43

Chapter 1
Author's Purpose

This chapter addresses the following Georgia Performance Standards for reading:

ELA6RC2	The student participates in discussions related to curricular learning in all subject areas. The student:
	e. Examines the author's purpose in writing.
ElA6RC4	The student establishes a context for information acquired by reading across subject areas. The student:
	a. Explores life experiences related to subject area content.

Think about the very last thing you read. What was your reason for reading? Were you reading a textbook to gather information for a school subject? Were you reading your favorite fiction author for entertainment? Were you reading someone's personal expressions?

This chapter will help you to gain some important concepts about reading for understanding. After reading this chapter, you will know how to identify an author's reason for writing.

AUTHOR'S PURPOSE

People read many types of literature every day. Some people begin the morning with a look at the local newspaper, while others like to end the day by reading a chapter from their favorite novel. When people read these different types of writing, they are reading with various aims in mind. Perhaps the morning newspaper reader wants to know what is going on in the community. Maybe the nightly novel reader is interested in reading for relaxation. What are some of the reasons that you read? Take a moment to discuss with a partner why you choose to read specific types of literature at given times.

Just as people read for different reasons, writers create literature with various aims or purposes in mind. An **author's purpose** is his or her reason for writing. Consider the following types of writing: a novel, a textbook chapter, a friendly letter, and an editorial. What do you think might be the reasons that writers would compose each of those types of literature? An author may have more than one purpose in mind when writing, but one purpose is usually the most important. In general, writers create literature for the purposes of **entertaining**, **informing**, **expressing**, or **persuading**. Let's explore what writing looks like in each of these four categories.

LITERATURE THAT ENTERTAINS

What would you read just for fun? Chances are, your choice of entertainment reading would be something that is funny, exciting, or perhaps has an element of mystery. When an author's purpose is **to entertain**, the writing is often fiction and follows a story line that makes readers want to tune in. Examples of literature for entertainment might be fiction books, short stories, humorous episodes, or graphic novels. Think also of the last movie you went to see. The story on the big screen started out as a written story that the author created for the purpose of entertaining the audience. Can you think of specific examples of writing that is meant to entertain?

Read the following, taken from *Dorothy and the Wizard in Oz* by L. Frank Baum. After reading, take a minute to discuss with a classmate the characteristics of the writing that make it entertaining.

The train from 'Frisco was very late. It should have arrived at Hugson's Siding at midnight, but it was already five o'clock and the gray dawn was breaking in the east when the little train slowly rumbled up to the open shed that served for the station-house. As it came to a stop the conductor called out in a loud voice:

"Hugson's Siding!"

At once a little girl rose from her seat and walked to the door of the car, carrying a wicker suit-case in one hand and a round bird-cage covered up with newspapers in the other, while a parasol was tucked under her arm. The conductor helped her off the car and then the engineer started his train again, so that it puffed and groaned and moved slowly away up the track. The reason he was so late was because all through the night there were times when the solid earth shook and trembled under him, and the engineer was afraid that at any moment the rails might spread apart and an accident happen to his passengers. So he moved the cars slowly and with caution.

The little girl stood still to watch until the train had disappeared around a curve; then she turned to see where she was.

As a reader, you might know that a passage such as this is for the purpose of entertainment because it is a fiction story. When writers write fiction, although it may be realistic, the events are made up. These made up events appeal to readers' imaginations. As readers read, images form in their minds, and they are drawn in to the world that the writer creates. Writing that entertains is useful both to teach readers about the world around them and to give readers the opportunity to use their imaginations.

LITERATURE THAT INFORMS

In addition to being entertaining, writing is a great way to share information. By reading, we learn about important events happening in the world around us. We can become informed about almost any topic. Many writers create literature for the purpose of **informing** readers.

Examples are your textbooks, scholarly journals, and newspapers. Textbooks inform readers in academic subjects such as literature, mathematics, science, and social studies. Newspapers keep readers up to speed on what is happening in the community, the country, and the world. Can you think of specific examples of writing in which an author's purpose is **to inform**?

Read the following passage from Booker T. Washington's autobiography *Up from Slavery*. Pay attention to the details about which he informs the reader.

Booker T. Washington

The early years of my life, which were spent in the little cabin, were not very different from those of thousands of other slaves. My mother, of course, had little time in which to give attention to the training of her children during the day. She snatched a few moments for our care in the early morning before her work began, and at night after the day's work was done. One of my earliest recollections is that of my mother cooking a chicken late at night, and awakening her children for the purpose of feeding them. How or where she got it I do not know. I presume, however, it was procured from our owner's farm. Some people may call this theft. If such a thing were to happen now, I should condemn it as theft myself. But taking place at the time it did, and for the reason that it did, no one could ever make me believe that my mother was guilty of thieving. She was simply a victim of the system of slavery.

As a reader, knowing that this is a work of nonfiction, you can expect to be informed about the conditions of life during the time of slavery. Since it is a passage that is autobiographical, you know that the details will inform you about Washington's life. By reading this passage, you learn that during the time of slavery, many slaves had a hard time finding food to eat by honest means. You learn that conditions were difficult.

LITERATURE THAT EXPRESSES

Writing is also an effective way to express oneself. Many authors create literature for the purpose of **expression** or communicating personal ideas. Perhaps they are expressing personal feelings as poets or journal writers. Sometimes, authors write **to express** opinions, such as writers of newspaper editorials. Can you think of some specific examples of writing that is meant to express thoughts or feelings?

Read the following poem. What key ideas are expressed about a lost thought?

> I FELT a clearing in my mind
>   As if my brain had split;
> I tried to match it, seam by seam,
>   But could not make them fit.
>
> The thought behind I strove to join
>   Unto the thought before,
> But sequence raveled out of reach
>   Like balls upon a floor.

–Emily Dickinson

This poem expresses what the speaker feels upon losing a thought. While it expresses a personal idea of the poet, the feeling is one that many people understand. In this way, writing that expresses personal feelings or ideas appeals to readers who may sometimes have these same feelings.

LITERATURE THAT PERSUADES

A final purpose for writing is **persuasion**. Authors writing **to persuade** want to influence or convince the reader about something. Examples of this type of writing might be advertisements for products and services or newspaper editorials. Persuasive writers who wish to sell a product will use strong words that are positive descriptors of their product. Sometimes, writers wish to change or influence the thinking of their readers. In this case, they often use strong statements to help sway the readers' thinking. They work hard to provide strong proof and evidence that will support the claims they make. Can you think of a specific example of writing where the author's purpose was to persuade? The following are some commonly used examples of persuasive writing:

- sales advertisements
- campaign speeches
- editorials
- political articles

Practice 1: Author's Purpose

Read each passage and decide if the author's purpose is to entertain, inform, express, or persuade.

> When writing an essay, it is always a good idea to use the writing process. The writing process is a series of steps used to create quality writing. It begins with brainstorming, the step during which the writer considers good ideas that could be developed into a strong essay.

1. These lines are taken from a passage in which the author's purpose is to

   A. entertain.   **B.** inform.   **C.** express.   **D.** persuade.

> Once upon a time there was a wicked sprite. Indeed, he was the most mischievous of all sprites. One day he was in a very good humor, for he had made a mirror with the power of causing all that was good and beautiful, when it was reflected therein, to look poor and mean…

   –from Hans Christian Andersen's "The Snow Queen"

2. These lines are taken from a passage in which the author's purpose is to

   A. entertain.   **B.** inform.   **C.** express.   **D.** persuade.

> I'm nobody! Who are you?
> Are you nobody, too?
> Then there's a pair of us—don't tell!
> They'd banish us, you know.
>
> How dreary to be somebody!
> How public, like a frog
> To tell your name the livelong day
> To an admiring bog!

   –Emily Dickinson

3. The author's purpose in writing this poem is to

   A. entertain.   **B.** inform.   **C.** express.   **D.** persuade.

Mr. Brown sells the toughest nails, hammers, and building supplies around town. Why go to those huge hardware stores that don't know how to treat the average customer, when you can get all you need for your home improvement jobs right at Mr. Brown's Downtown Hardware store? Located in downtown Smithville, Mr. Brown's is the place to go for good prices, good, quality equipment, and good service. Stop by and see Mr. Brown today!

4. The author's purpose in writing this advertisement is to

   A. entertain.   **B.** inform.   **C.** express.   **D.** persuade.

CONTEXT FOR READING

Just as there are many reasons for writing, there are many reasons for reading and studying literature. One reason is to explore and better understand your own life. Strong readers can relate story events to real life. They learn something from what characters go through. This is called having a **context for reading**. Your own life becomes the context!

For example, think of a story about two good friends. How they relate can teach a reader how to build strong relationships. Now, think of a story about a character who has to overcome an obstacle and is successful. This story can encourage a reader to do the same. In this same way, you can use personal experiences to better understand what you read.

Practice 2: Context for Reading

Read the excerpts, and answer the questions that follow.

> It was the first day of school. Brandy's stomach was a mess of knots and nervous flutter. As she approached the large campus of Gilmer Middle School, she did her best not to make direct contact with anyone. Trying not to let her face show what her mind thought, Brandy could not quiet the questions to herself: *Are my clothes alright*? *Will I get lost today*? *What if I don't make new friends*? There was just no telling what was ahead.

1. Based upon what you know about young pre-teens and managing disappointment, which of the following is **most likely** to occur?

   A. to see her mother waiting at the front door to escort her through school

   B. to lose her footing and trip, falling to the ground

   C. to meet a nice friend who can give her some help or at least chat with her

   D. to continue through the day nervous and alone

Her world was ending. Nicole could not believe that she would be confined to remain within the four walls of her bedroom on the weekend when her best friend, Amaya was having *their* birthday party. Every year since they were four years old, Nicole and Amaya had shared a birthday party. It was the most exciting time of the year for Nicole. There were always friends, food, and fun. This time, though, Nicole would be stuck in her room, forced to study for the re-take of the science test she had just bombed. Could her life be any worse right now? What was the fun of a twelfth birthday if there was no party to celebrate?

2. Based upon what you know about young pre-teens and managing disappointment, which of the following is **most likely** to occur?

   A. On her own, Nicole might settle down and realize that a science test is more important than a birthday party.

   B. Nicole might cry herself to sleep thast night.

   C. Nicole might sneak out of her second story window to get to the party.

   D. Nicole might forget all about the party and realize that she likes science more.

CHAPTER 1 SUMMARY

Author's Purpose – An author's purpose is his or her reason for writing. In general, writers create literature for the purposes of entertaining, informing, expressing, or persuading.

- **Literature that entertains** – This type of literature is created for the enjoyment of the reader. This generally refers to fiction. It may contain elements of action, adventure, and mystery.

- **Literature that informs** – This type of literature is written for the purpose of giving the reader information. For example, newspaper articles and textbooks are written to inform.

- **Literature that expresses** – This type of literature expresses the personal ideas or feelings of a writer.

- **Literature that persuades** – This type of literature is written to convince or influence a reader.

Context for reading – There are many reasons to read and study literature. One is to learn more about yourself and relate stories to your own life.

CHAPTER 1 REVIEW

Read each passage and identify the author's purpose.

Englishman Lewis Carroll lived from 1832 to 1898. Among his many activities, Lewis Carroll was an author, educator, preacher, and mathematician. Born in Daresbury in Cheshire, he belonged to a wealthy and large family. Carroll's early formal education took place at the Yorkshire Grammar School. Later, while attending Christ Church in Oxford, he studied mathematics while working as a lecturer. Despite his talent in mathematics, Carroll's career as an educator was limited by his tendency to stammer. Even so, he did do some lecturing and even preaching throughout the course of his career.

1. The author's purpose is to

    A. entertain.   **B.** inform.   **C.** persuade.   **D.** express.

Alice was beginning to get very tired of sitting by her sister on the bank, and of having nothing to do: once or twice she had peeped into the book her sister was reading, but it had no pictures or conversations in it, "and what is the use of a book," thought Alice "without pictures or conversation?"

–from *Alice's Adventures in Wonderland*
by Lewis Carroll

2. The author's purpose is to

    A. entertain.   **B.** inform.   **C.** persuade.   **D.** express.

Today was a very good day. I went to school, where we had field day exercises and got to miss math. We had cheeseburgers, my favorite, for lunch. After school, Mom and Dad took Jenna and me to see a movie. I wish every day could be so much fun.

3. The author's purpose is to

    A. entertain.   **B.** inform.   **C.** persuade.   **D.** express.

For great values and quality foods, do your shopping at Value Market. Our stores are clean and neat and offer unbeatable prices. Why shop anywhere else? No one beats Value Market.

4. The author's purpose is to

    A. entertain.   **B.** inform.   **C.** persuade.   **D.** express.

It is not good to waste the resources of the earth or to contaminate the earth. When you brush your teeth and let the water run, you are wasting water. When you pour liquids containing harmful chemicals down the drain, you are polluting. When you use aerosol sprays and waste energy, you are damaging the earth. If we all would do our share to conserve resources and keep the earth clean, it would make a safer and healthier future for us all. Everyone should do his or her part to care for the earth.

5. The author's purpose is to

    A. entertain.   **B.** inform.   **C.** persuade.   **D.** express.

There was once a Prince who wished to marry a Princess; but then she must be a real Princess. He traveled all over the world in hopes of finding such a lady; but there was always something wrong. Princesses he found in plenty; but whether they were real Princesses it was impossible for him to decide, for now one thing, now another, seemed to him not quite right about the ladies. At last he returned to his palace quite cast down, because he wished so much to have a real Princess for his wife.

–from Hans Christian Andersen's "The Real Princess"

6. The author's purpose is to

    A. entertain.   **B.** inform.   **C.** persuade.   **D.** express.

Hans Christian Andersen

Hans Christian Andersen was born in Odense, Denmark. He was the son of a shoe-maker and a washerwoman. They were very poor. While growing up, Andersen had many personal tragedies. His father died while he was young, and many of his peers rejected him. Despite his struggles and the fact that he received little education, Andersen grew up to become a world renowned author and poet.

7. The author's purpose is to

   A. entertain.   **B.** inform.   **C.** persuade.   **D.** express.

Langston Hughes

Langston Hughes, who lived from 1902 to 1967, was an African American poet, essayist, and dramatist. He wrote during the Harlem Renaissance era. He was born in Joplin, Missouri, into a family that was well known for abolition and civil activism. Despite the disapproval of his father and some other family members, Hughes began writing poetry in the eighth grade. In his journey through life, Hughes found his voice through writing about the struggles and experiences of the African American. He also sought to be recognized for who he was, not what color he was.

8. The author's purpose is to

   A. entertain.   **B.** inform.   **C.** persuade.   **D.** express.

We're queer folks here
    We'll talk about the weather,
     The good times we've had together
The good times near,
    The roses buddin', an' the bees
    Once more upon their nectar sprees;
    The scarlet fever scare, an' who
    Came mighty near not pullin' through,
    An' who had light attacks, an' all
    The things that int'rest, big or small;
But here you'll never hear of sinnin'
Or any scandal that's beginnin'.
We've got too many other labors
To scatter tales that harm our neighbors.

–from Edgar A. Guest's "Just Folks"

9. The author's purpose is to

   A. entertain.   **B.** inform.   **C.** persuade.   **D.** express.

Many years ago, there was an Emperor, who was so excessively fond of new clothes, that he spent all his money in dress. He did not trouble himself in the least about his soldiers; nor did he care to go either to the theatre or the chase, except for the opportunities then afforded him for displaying his new clothes. He had a different suit for each hour of the day; and as of any other king or emperor, one is accustomed to say, "he is sitting in council," it was always said of him, "The Emperor is sitting in his wardrobe."

–from Hans Christian Andersen's "The Emperor's New Clothes"

10. The author's purpose is to

   A. entertain.   **B.** inform.   **C.** persuade.   **D.** express.

The Ant and the Grasshopper

In a field one summer's day, a Grasshopper was hopping about, chirping and singing to its heart's content. An Ant passed by, bearing along with great toil an ear of corn he was taking to the nest.

"Why not come and chat with me," said the Grasshopper, "instead of toiling and moiling in that way?"

"I am helping to lay up food for the winter," said the Ant, "and I recommend you to do the same."

"Why bother about winter?" said the Grasshopper. "We have got plenty of food at present." But the Ant went on its way and continued its toil. When the winter came, the Grasshopper had no food and found itself dying of hunger, while it saw the ants distributing every day corn and grain from the stores they had collected in the summer. Then the Grasshopper knew:

It is best to prepare for the days of necessity.

–from Aesop's fables

11. Which of the following experiences would **best** help you to understand why the ants worked so hard all summer?

    A. doing homework even when you want to play, so that you can earn a good grade

    B. failing at something and getting punished by being grounded or not getting something you want

    C. playing during a time when you should have been working

    D. learning to do something that is very difficult

12. Think about people that you know. What kind of person is the grasshopper **most** like?

    A. The grasshopper is like a teacher, always helping other people learn what to do.

    B. The grasshopper is like a best friend, helping you get things accomplished.

    C. The grasshopper is like a distracting classmate, keeping you from doing your work.

    D. The grasshopper is like a parent, giving you advice about life.

Chapter 2
Paragraph Structure and Main Idea

This chapter addresses the following Georgia Performance Standards for reading:

ELA6R1	The student demonstrates comprehension and shows evidence of a warranted and responsible explanation of a variety of literary and informational texts.
	For informational texts, the student reads and comprehends in order to develop understanding and expertise and produces evidence of reading that:
	a. Applies knowledge of common textual features (e.g., paragraphs, topic sentences, concluding sentences…).
	d. Identifies and analyzes main ideas, supporting ideas, and supporting details.

In chapter 1, you learned how to recognize the author's purpose for writing different types of literature. This chapter is about literature that is meant to inform and literature that is meant to entertain. You will learn how to recognize the parts of a paragraph and how to identify main ideas. Let's begin with a look at paragraph structure.

PARAGRAPHS

Have you ever built something or watched it being built? Perhaps you have assembled a Lego™ tower or something similar. Perhaps you observed over time as a new house or subdivision was being constructed. In each case, you will probably remember that the

builder started with very little—a foundation—then added support and lastly filled in the frame to make a complete and solid structure. In writing novels, short stories, and informational texts, writers go through a similar process, beginning with an idea, adding support, and finally filling in detail to create a complete work. In writing of any sort, **paragraphs** are the building blocks. A series of paragraphs together makes up the complete text.

Within most paragraphs, there are these elements: **topic sentences**, **main ideas**, **supporting ideas and details**, and **concluding sentences**.

MAIN IDEA

Every paragraph has a **main idea**. The main idea is the big idea that is the focus of the entire paragraph. It is the most important idea in the paragraph. Read the following paragraph, keeping an eye out for the main idea.

> Many students feel that they are assigned too much homework. To spend one or two hours a weekday working on school assignments, after having attended school for six or more hours, seems to be excessive. Students feel that schoolwork should be done in school, and only in school. Time away from school should be reserved for recreation, family, and friends. These students believe that teachers assigning work to be done at home is an unfair and inconsiderate practice. While many students feel that they are assigned too much homework, when it comes down to being good students, they have no choice but to complete the assignments.

After reading, you were probably able to decide that the main idea of the paragraph was stated in this sentence:

> Many students feel that they are assigned too much homework.

TOPIC SENTENCE

This sentence, which states the main idea, or topic of the paragraph, is called the **topic sentence**.

In a paragraph, the topic sentence is usually found near the beginning. It is often the first sentence. However, it also may be at or near the end. When you are reading, to spot topic sentences, you must ask yourself, "What is this paragraph about?" The sentence that answers this question is the topic sentence.

SUPPORTING IDEAS AND DETAILS

We have already decided that the main idea, as stated by the topic sentence, is that many students feel that they are assigned too much homework. Now, read the paragraph again. Think about what ideas and details support the main idea as you look at the paragraph again.

After rereading the paragraph, what do you say are the **supporting ideas and details**?

If you chose the sentences below, then you are on the right track to understanding supporting ideas and details. Supporting ideas and details add information about the main idea of a paragraph. They help the reader to understand the focus presented by the topic sentence.

- To spend one or two hours a week day working on school assignments after having attended school for six or more hours seems to be excessive.
- They feel that schoolwork should be done in school, and only in school.
- Time away from school should be reserved for recreation, family, and friends.
- These students feel that teachers assigning work to be done at home is an unfair and inconsiderate practice.

Supporting ideas and details are used to expand the main idea of a paragraph. They offer more information to help the reader understand the paragraph's focus. Without supporting details, a paragraph does not offer a reader enough information.

CONCLUDING SENTENCES

Look at the paragraph one more time. Can you identify the **concluding sentence**? It is the sentence that sums up the whole paragraph and perhaps makes a broad and general statement. Usually, it is the last sentence of a paragraph. The concluding sentence brings the paragraph to a close by restating the main idea and often adding a general statement to encourage thinking.

After rereading the paragraph, what did you say is the **concluding sentence**?

If you identified this sentence, then you understand that the concluding sentence of a paragraph wraps it all up for the reader:

> While many students feel that they are assigned too much homework, when it comes down to being good students, they have no choice but to complete the assignments.

Practice 1: Identifying Sentences in a Paragraph

Read the paragraph. Then identify the **topic sentence**, **supporting idea/detail sentences**, and the **concluding sentence**.

(1) There are many great places to vacation. **(2)** For example, beach resorts offer beautiful landscapes and ample opportunities for recreational fun. **(3)** There is usually plenty of sand, sun, and water for sporting. **(4)** Also, historic regions often have breathtaking sights while offering travelers educational highlights. **(5)** Jamestown, Virginia, is an example of a historic area that attracts annual vacationers. **(6)** Finally, theme parks offer vacationers thrilling attractions that are enjoyable for the whole family. **(7)** Six Flags, Busch Gardens, and Kings Dominion are a few examples of theme parks that travelers love to visit and enjoy. **(8)** As one can see, vacation options are virtually endless—a sense of adventure and a destination is all one needs to plan and enjoy a fabulous vacation.

1. Which of the following sentences is the topic sentence?

   A. Sentence 1   **B.** Sentence 4   **C.** Sentence 6   **D.** Sentence 7

2. Which set is comprised of all supporting idea/detail sentences?

   A. Sentences 1, 2, 3   **C.** Sentences 1, 6, 8

   B. Sentences 3, 5, 7   **D.** Sentences 6, 7, 8

3. Which of the following sentences is the concluding sentence?

   A. Sentence 1   **B.** Sentence 4   **C.** Sentence 6   **D.** Sentence 8

RECOGNIZING HIDDEN MAIN IDEAS IN INFORMATIONAL TEXTS

Sometimes, when you are reading an informational text, there is no clear topic sentence that states the main idea. Rather, the **main idea** is **implied**. This means that you, as the reader, are responsible for deciding the main idea of the paragraph. In other cases, the paragraph contains a topic sentence that is embedded; perhaps it is not the first sentence.

Tips for Finding the Main Idea
1. **Read** the paragraph carefully.
2. **Look** for ideas that occur in many of the sentences.
3. **Ask** yourself how you would summarize the paragraph in your own words if you could only make a one-sentence statement. This sentence is the overall main idea.

Read the following paragraph.

Lights, people everywhere, the hustle and bustle of the city—the winter holiday season is upon us. Family gatherings, breaks from school, and holiday television specials are all characteristic of the season. For some, it is a time of sharing and excitement. It is a welcome season to which one looks forward. For others, it is a time of stress and stretched budgets. What does the winter holiday season mean to you?

While reading this paragraph, perhaps you were not able to identify a clear **topic sentence**, but what ideas occur in many of the sentences? Can you make a clear topic sentence that would fit the paragraph details? If you said something like this, then you are on the right track:

> The holiday season is a busy time of year that excites some but is stressful for others.

This sentence states the main idea of the paragraph.

Practice 2: Recognizing Hidden Main Ideas

Read the paragraph and choose the sentence that best states the main idea.

When one is too old for some childhood games, yet not old enough to be a part of adult activities, the time is young adolescence. The world is fun and exciting, yet still large and looming. As they enter middle school and leave behind the comfort and security of elementary hallways, 10-year-olds learn to change classes and memorize locker combinations. Outside of school, there are new interests, such as social rather than family circles. They become aware of personal style and begin the struggle of finding their places in the world. Young adolescence is a time of change.

1. Which of the following sentences **best** states the main idea of this paragraph?

    A. Young adolescence is a time to celebrate the change from childhood to adolescence.

    B. During adolescence, young people become focused on friends rather than family.

    C. Young adolescence is a time of change.

    D. There are new interests available.

Read the following passage, and see if you can determine its main idea.

The sun shone brightly across the mesh table where Daphne sat in front of a small Italian bistro waiting for the sight of a blue minivan that would mean Rochelle's mom was on the way with Rochelle. Rochelle and Daphne had been friends since the first grade. They had been mat mates in kindergarten and Girl Scout troopers in first grade. In the fourth grade, they were a hall monitor team, and now, as sixth, soon-to-be seventh graders, they were having their first movie day out together without parents.

Looking around her, Daphne noticed the movement of the shopping center. Cars rolled slowly around the Starbuck's drive-thru. From where she sat, Daphne could hear their detailed orders. For a moment, she wondered what it would be like to be one of those drivers, at the wheel of her own pink Jeep Wrangler. She watched as mothers went with their daughters into the Limited Too, thinking how exciting it was to be out at the plaza, not on the arm of her own mom, although mom was just across the boulevard at the next shopping plaza, calling her every couple of minutes to see if Rochelle had arrived.

Daphne thought about how they would spend the Sunday afternoon. They would watch a movie at the Regal Cinema and get a cheeseburger afterwards. It would be just like they were high schoolers, she thought. They would spend their own money and have things their way. It was going to be a good day.

2. Which sentence **best** expresses the main idea?

    A. Daphne and Rochelle have been friends for a very long time.

    B. Daphne is excited about the freedom of a day out with her friend Rochelle.

    C. Rochelle has much more fun in life than Daphne, even though they are best friends.

    D. Daphne does not want to be accompanied everywhere she goes by her mom anymore.

What would we do without it? Even today, people use letter writing as a form of communication. Think of the many forms in which it now exists. Email, or electronic mail, uses the computer to expedite the letter-writing process. "Snail mail," which has become a synonym for mail delivered through postal courier services, still exists, too. Not only do regular mail-delivery services still exist, but they are a viable form of communication for citizens and businesses everywhere.

3. Which of the following sentences **best** states the main idea of this paragraph?

   A. Regular mail courier services are called "snail mail," while computer mail is called electronic mail.

   B. Letter writing now exists in the form of email.

   C. We couldn't function as a society if we did not write letters.

   D. Letter writing is still a form of communication and includes both email and "snail mail."

CHAPTER 2 SUMMARY

- **Paragraphs** are the building blocks of writing.

- Every paragraph has a **main idea**. The main idea is the big idea that is the focus of the entire paragraph. It is the most important idea in the paragraph. The sentence which states the main idea, or topic of the paragraph, is called the **topic sentence**.

- **Supporting ideas and details** explain and back up the main idea. They help the reader to understand the idea presented by the topic sentence.

- The **concluding sentence** is usually the last sentence of a paragraph. It brings the paragraph to a close by summarizing the main idea.

- Sometimes, the main idea is not stated. Here are some tips to help you find the **hidden main idea**:

  - Read the paragraph carefully.

  - Look for ideas that occur in many of the sentences.

  - Ask yourself how you would summarize the paragraph in your own words if you could only make a one-sentence statement. This sentence is the hidden main idea.

CHAPTER 2 REVIEW

For each of the following, read the paragraph. Then answer the questions that follow.

> **(1)** Effective writing requires good content, strong style, and proper form. **(2)** Good content in writing means that a writer has strong ideas that are adequately supported by facts, examples, and details. **(3)** Ideas must be clearly presented and given enough explanation for the reader to understand. **(4)** Strong style is another important element in effective writing. Each writer has a unique way of using words. **(5)** This signature technique is known as style. **(6)** Style is what adds an element of interest for the reader. Finally, proper form, which refers to a writer's grammar, is important. **(7)** Grammatical errors cause reading difficulty and take away from a reader's understanding. **(8)** It is clear that, in order for writing to be effective, a writer must pay attention to the elements of content, style, and form.

1. Which sentence states the main idea?

    A. Sentence 1 **B.** Sentence 2 **C.** Sentence 4 **D.** Sentence 8

2. Which of the following is **not** a supporting idea/detail?

    A. Sentence 3 **B.** Sentence 2 **C.** Sentence 4 **D.** Sentence 8

3. Which of the following is the concluding sentence?

    A. Sentence 1 **B.** Sentence 3 **C.** Sentence 5 **D.** Sentence 8

> **(1)** Active readers have strong techniques that help them to comprehend and find personal associations with what they read. **(2)** One technique that active readers use is highlighting. **(3)** Active readers highlight words they don't know and phrases that jump out at them. **(4)** Another technique of active readers is margin notes.

> **(5)** In the margins of the text, they write notes to themselves about what unfamiliar words mean and personal connections they make with what they read. **(6)** These techniques enable active readers to get the most out of everything they read.

4. Which sentence is the topic sentence?

    A. Sentence 1 **B.** Sentence 2 **C.** Sentence 3 **D.** Sentence 4

5. Which sentence is **not** a supporting idea/detail?

    A. Sentence 1 **B.** Sentence 2 **C.** Sentence 3 **D.** Sentence 4

6. Which sentence is the concluding sentence?

    A. Sentence 1   **B.** Sentence 2   **C.** Sentence 4   **D.** Sentence 6

Read the following paragraphs that do not contain clearly stated main ideas. Look for clues to help you decide on good possible main ideas for the paragraphs.

Good students study regularly. Regular studying means that one will have a better chance to retain material, rather than to simply memorize it. Good students also understand that being organized helps to streamline homework time, class note taking, and test review sessions. Good students also have study buddies for note sharing when they are away from school. This ensures that they do not miss assignments and important information given out during class. These students attend teacher help sessions and ask questions when they do not understand.

7. Which of the following sentences **best** states the main idea of the paragraph?

    A. There are many good middle school students.

    B. Teachers appreciate students who work hard and ask questions.

    C. Good students have strong habits at home and at school.

    D. There is no way to clearly identify a good student.

Healthy eating is one aspect of maintaining health. Eating lots of fruits and vegetables, drinking water, and being careful of one's sugary, fatty food intake are some ways to eat healthfully. Another way to maintain health is to exercise several times a week. Exercise helps to promote blood circulation and strong bone health. Getting adequate sleep is yet another important aspect of healthful living. Most people need seven to eight hours of uninterrupted sleep time nightly.

8. Which of the following sentences **best** states the main idea of the paragraph?

    A. There are many options for healthy eating.

    B. Most people do not get enough sleep.

    C. It is important to exercise regularly.

    D. There are several aspects of healthy living.

In most areas of the country, weather is a concern for the homeless. Temperature extremes of both heat and cold present a problem for those living on the streets. From day to day, they also have the difficulty of obtaining adequate food and shelter, often being without the resource of money. Crime is an issue; many homeless people find themselves relegated to seedy urban areas where they are able to blend in to a backdrop of poverty and busy street life. Unfortunately, those who are homeless are also jobless. Therefore, besides the obvious, they also lack adequate services for physical and psychiatric health care.

9. Which of the following sentences **best** states the main idea of the paragraph?

   A. Weather is a concern for those who are homeless.

   B. Food and shelter is a concern for America's homeless.

   C. The life of a homeless American citizen is filled with hardship.

   D. Homeless citizens are responsible for many violent and non-violent crimes.

Many students think they can remember assignments, class reminders, and due dates without the help of writing them down. Rather than using school-issued planners, they rely upon memory and the responsible behavior of class friends to help them stay on the task. Often, these same students will miss important due dates and fail to turn in assignments on time. When tests are given, these students will arrive in class and ask the infamous question, "Oh, do we have a test today?" Such incidents could be avoided if these students made proper use of their planners.

10. Which of the following sentences **best** states the main idea of the paragraph?

   A. Student planners are an optional organizational tool.

   B. Some students could be more successful and better organized through the consistent use of planners.

   C. Students who do not use planners should be given detention.

   D. Students who do not use their planners to record important dates and assignments are unsuccessful in school.

Chapter 3
Structure and Patterns in Writing

This chapter addresses the following Georgia Performance Standards for reading:

ELA6R1	The student demonstrates comprehension and shows evidence of a warranted and responsible explanation of a variety of literary and informational texts.
	For informational texts, the student reads and comprehends in order to develop understanding and expertise and produces evidence of reading that:
	c. Applies knowledge of common organizational structures and patterns (e.g., transitions, logical order, cause and effect, classification schemes).

In chapter 2, you learned about the parts of a paragraph. In this chapter, you will extend that lesson and learn about ways that writers organize their writing. Writers use **organizational patterns** so that their writing makes sense to the reader. The following sections explain structures and tools that writers commonly use for organization.

TRANSITIONS

One tool that writers use to create structure is the transition. **Transitions** may be individual words, or they may be phrases. Transitions show that ideas are connected and how they are connected. Transitions help readers to understand what they read. They act as signals for how ideas go together. Familiarize yourself with the following explanations and lists of commonly used transitional words and phrases.

SEQUENCE OF EVENTS

When writers use **sequence of events**, they arrange the details of a story in the order in which they happened. This is also called **time order.** Sequence of events can go from the first to the last event or from the last to the first event. Usually, stories will be arranged from the first to the last event. Think of the last time friends told you a

personal story. Did they use time order? Did they tell the story from the first to the last event or the other way around? Below are some transition words and phrases that are often used to show a sequence of events.

Sequence of Events Transitions			
after	before	first	then
at last	eventually	meanwhile	thereafter
at once	finally	next	when

Practice 1:   Sequence of Events Transitions

Read the passage and answer the questions that follow.

One Monday morning, Missy awoke not feeling well at all. She was hot, and her throat was dry and scratchy. "Oh, no," she thought. "What about the book fair?" Missy had been chosen to be a fair monitor for her class. Her job would be to help bag student purchases and keep an eye on the lines. She had been looking forward to this day for two weeks. While Missy lay there hoping she wasn't very sick, she heard her mother calling from down below.

 "Missy, time to get up." Upon hearing her mother's call, Missy got up from her bed, feeling groggy. Yet, she was determined to get to school for the day. After getting cleaned up and dressed for school, Missy went down for breakfast. Looking at the breakfast her mother had prepared, she still felt a little woozy. Then, she said to her mother, "I'm really not very hungry. I think I will just have some juice today." Missy's mother found this strange because her daughter was known to love her daily bacon and eggs breakfast.

"Missy, are you feeling okay?" she inquired, touching the back of her right hand to Missy's warm forehead. "Oh dear," she exclaimed, "you're burning up. Let me get the thermometer." Just then, Missy heard the school bus approaching the corner. As her mom left the room, Missy jumped up.

Breaking into a jog, she yelled back to her mother, "Mom, I'm fine. I was just feeling a little hot because I slept under the heavy comforter all night. I feel great...gotta' go." And with that, she bounded out the door, just in time to reach the approaching school bus at its stop. By that time, her mother arrived waving the thermometer and looking for her.

"But wait," she called to Missy, who was waving out from the moving bus' window, "I wanted to check..." Her mom's voice trailed off as she watched, now only able to see the back of the bus as it pulled away from the bus stop.

1. Which of the following events happens first?

    A. Missy thought about missing her turn as fair monitor.

    B. Missy awoke not feeling well.

    C. Missy's mother ran out of the room to get the thermometer.

    D. Missy ran out the door to catch the bus.

2. Which of the following events happens last?

    A. Missy thought about missing her turn as fair monitor.

    B. Missy awoke not feeling well.

    C. Missy's mother ran out of the room to get the thermometer.

    D. Missy ran out the door to catch the bus.

3. What is the purpose of the transition *while* in this sentence?

    > *While* Missy lay there hoping she wasn't very sick, she heard her mother calling from down below.

    A. It shows that Missy was lying in bed before she became sick.

    B. It shows that Missy was went to bed after she became sick.

    C. It shows that Missy was lying in bed during the time she felt sick.

    D. *While* is not used as a transition in this sentence.

Reread paragraph 2 from the passage. Answer the questions that follow.

> "Missy, time to get up." Upon hearing her mother's call, Missy got up from her bed, feeling groggy. Yet, she was determined to get to school for the day. After getting cleaned up and dressed for school, Missy went down for breakfast. Looking at the breakfast her mother had prepared, she still felt a little woozy. Then, she said to her mother, "I'm really not very hungry. I think I will just have some juice today." Missy's mother found this strange because her daughter was known to love her daily bacon and eggs breakfast.

4. Which of the following words from the paragraph is a transition word that helps to show a sequence of events?

    A. actually   **B.** after   **C.** because   **D.** today

5. Which of the following words from the paragraph is used as a transition word to help explain when events from the passage occur?

    A. actually   **B.** yet   **C.** because   **D.** upon

CAUSE AND EFFECT

Cause and effect is another organizational structure that writers use. Cause and effect shows how events in a story relate to one another. A **cause** makes something happen. An **effect** is what happens due to the cause. What is the cause/effect relationship between good diet and health? What is the cause/effect relationship between poor study habits and poor grades? What other cause/effect relationships can you think of? The following are transitional words and phrases that are often used to show cause and effect:

Cause and Effect Transitions			
accordingly	consequently	hence	therefore
as a result	due to	so	thus
because	for that reason	so that	why

Practice 2: Cause/Effect Transitions

Read the following passage and answer the questions that follow.

It was Friday afternoon, and instead of being out with friends, Jake stared longingly out the window at the group of neighborhood boys gathered for a game of toss and tag football. "Humph," he thought to himself as he watched a wobbly ball slowly making its way thorough the air. "I could have thrown that much straighter." In the distance, he could see the early evening sun hanging in the sky. It was such a nice, autumn day—not too hot or cold, just right to play outside. If only he had studied and passed that math test earlier. Instead of studying, he had spent several afternoons riding dirt bikes with the Marshall twins from two doors down. Now, he thought, he was stuck in the house, grounded for the weekend. Some things just weren't fair.

1. What causes Jake to stare longingly out of the window?

   A. The sun provides nice warmth for an autumn afternoon.

   B. He sees his brother playing out there.

   C. He wishes he could play football with the other boys.

   D. none of these

2. Which of the following sentences **best** makes a cause/effect statement about Jake's decision not to study and his poor performance on the test? Pay attention to the transition word choice.

   A. As a result of his decision not to study, Jake did not feel like playing football.

   B. Jake did not study for his math test; therefore, he did poorly.

   C. Jake did not get to play football, so he did poorly on his math test.

   D. Jake did poorly on his math test because he did not play with his friends.

CLASSIFICATION SCHEMES AND LOGICAL ORDER

Sometimes writers use **classification** to organize ideas. Classification means categorizing based upon similarities. For example, how would you organize the following animals: Labrador retriever, Siamese cat, cow, horse, shark, and whale? One way to organize them would be as follows:

Domestic Pets	Farm Animals	Sea Creatures
Labrador retriever	cow	shark
Siamese cat	horse	whale

When writers use classification schemes, they usually use some sort of **logical order**. Logical order makes sense to the reader and has a clear pattern. **Definition** and **comparison/contrast** are two common types of logical order that writers use when they classify information.

DEFINITION

When writers introduce new subjects to readers, they use **definition**. Definition in writing means to tell about a subject that is new to the reader.

Some transitions that signal definition include the following:

Definition Transitions		
equals	is	means
includes	is the same as	works like

COMPARISON AND CONTRAST

Writers also use **comparison and contrast** to organize ideas. When writers compare and contrast ideas, they show how these ideas are both alike and different. For example, how would you compare and contrast skateboarding and bicycle riding? What about middle school and elementary school?

Below are some transitions that are commonly used for comparison and contrast.

Comparing Ideas Transitions			
also	another	like	similarly
and	in addition	likewise	too

Contrasting Ideas Transitions		
but	not	unlike
however	on the other hand	while

Practice 3: Identifying Transitions

Read the passages and answer the questions that follow.

Dieting means having a special selection of food. Dieting has been around for thousands of years but became an organized concept sometime in the 1800s. It is one way that many people attempt to control, prevent, and correct health and weight issues. Some people choose to adopt an overall healthy eating lifestyle. This means that, rather than identify a specific selection of foods, these people eat what they want from a choice of healthy foods. Generally, people diet to meet personal and specific health goals. For example, some people have a diet of reduced fat. Usually, these people are trying to lose weight. Sometimes, to aid in health issues, like diabetes, people must reduce their sugar intake. To do this, they must stick to a diet that is low in sugar.

1. The writer's purpose in this paragraph is **most** likely

   A. definition.

   B. comparison.

   C. contrast.

   D. comparison and contrast.

2. Which word in the following sentence is a transition word that indicates contrasting ideas?

> Dieting has been around for thousands of years but became an organized concept sometime in the 1800s.

A. for　　　　　**B.** but　　　　　**C.** became　　　　　**D.** in

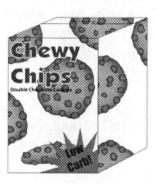

3. Which word in the following sentence is a transition that shows a comparison of ideas?

> Sometimes, to aid in health issues, like diabetes, people must reduce their sugar intake.

A. to　　　　　**B.** in　　　　　**C.** like　　　　　**D.** must

4. Which word or phrase in the following sentence is a transition that points to a definition?

> This means that, rather than identify a specific selection of foods, these people eat what they want from a choice of healthy foods.

A. this means　　　**B.** rather than　　　**C.** what　　　**D.** from

CHAPTER 3 SUMMARY

Transitions

One tool that writers use to create structure is **transitions**. Transitions may be individual words, or they may be phrases. Transitions show that ideas are connected and how they are connected. Transitions help readers to understand what they read. They act as signals for ideas that connect together.

Sequence of Events

When writers use **sequence of events**, they arrange the details of a story in the order in which they happened. This is also called **time order**. Sequence of events can go from the first to the last event or from the last to the first event.

Cause and Effect

Cause and effect is another organizational structure that writers use. Cause and effect shows how events in a story relate to one another. A **cause** makes something happen. An **effect** is what happens due to the cause.

Classification Schemes and Logical Order

Sometimes writers use classification to organize ideas. **Classification** means categorizing based upon similarities.

Definition

When writers introduce new subjects to readers, they use **definition**. Definition in writing means to tell about a subject that is new to the reader.

Comparison and Contrast

Writers use **comparison and contrast** to organize ideas. When writers compare, they show how ideas or things are similar. When they contrast, they show how these ideas or things are different.

CHAPTER 3 REVIEW

Read each passage and answer the questions that follow.

The bell rang and Carlie rushed out of the class. Hoping to make it to Spanish before Regina could get there, Carlie decided not to go to her locker. As she moved quickly, pushing her way through the sea of sixth graders all going the same direction, Carlie felt small. Finally, after a good bit of shouldering, dodging, and nudging, she stood outside of Senora Rodriguez's door, panting and out of breath. "Phew," she thought. She had made it there first. Regina wouldn't have a chance to steal the seat that Carlie wanted beside Gino. Just then, she turned to see a boy and a girl walking arm and arm down the hallway. They were laughing and being shadowed by a huddle of other kids. Could it be? *It was*! Regina and Gino were headed toward the door, arms linked, eyes locked, smiles matching. Carlie's heart sank. Just then, Senora Rodriguez appeared at the door. "*Buenos tardes*," she said with a warm smile. "*¿Cómo estás*?" Carlie didn't answer. She wasn't sure how to say "heartbroken" in Spanish.

1. In this passage, which of the following happens first?

   A. Carlie sees Gino and Regina on the way to Spanish.

   B. Carlie decides not to go to her locker.

   C. Carlie pushes her way through the crowd.

   D. Senora Rodriguez greets Carlie at the door.

2. In this passage, which of the following happens last?

   A. Carlie sees Gino and Regina on the way to Spanish.

   B. Carlie decides not to go to her locker.

   C. Carlie pushes her way through the crowd.

   D. Senora Rodriguez greets Carlie at the door.

Evan was tired. He had stayed up late last night playing computer games with his cousin, Josh. He had slept on the bus going to school. He had even slept through homeroom. Now, it was time for social studies, and Evan felt a yawn coming on. Looking up, he could see Mrs. Findley setting up for a class period of lecture and notes. "Oh boy," he groaned to himself, "this looks like it is going to be boring!" That was the last thing he remembered before… Evan heard a titter from the back of the room. It started as just one. Then, it became two, three, then a class full of giggling students. What was so funny? What was going on? It suddenly occurred to Evan that he had his head on the desk, and his eyes were closed. His arms were stretched out, hanging off either side of the desk. Oh no…had he been sleeping? "Mr. Harris?" Ms. Findley's tone, coming from above him and to his right, was both a question and an accusation. Evan knew this event would go down in his book of most embarrassing middle school moments.

3. In this passage, which of the following happens first?

   A. Evan stays up late at night.

   B. Evan sleeps on the bus because he played games into the night.

   C. Evan sleeps in homeroom.

   D. Ms. Findley catches Evan sleeping and embarrasses him.

4. In this passage, which of the following happens last?

   A. Evan stays up late at night.

   B. Evan sleeps on the bus because he played games into the night.

   C. Evan sleeps in homeroom.

   D. Ms. Findley catches Evan sleeping and embarrasses him.

Mrs. Kim looked out the window where the early morning sun shone through. She sat down on the couch for her daily cup of tea and meditations. As she did so, she heard a strange noise from the back of the house. Feeling a little alarmed, she looked around for a weapon just as Snickers, the family dog, began to bark. "Oh no," she thought as she really became nervous. The only thing that she could find was Richie's play golf club. How silly she felt creeping toward the back holding Richie's golf club above her head. Still, she moved quickly, as quietly as she could in her fuzzy slippers, to the back of the house. "Boo!" There was a scream from Mrs. Kim as she lowered the blow over Mr. Kim's head with a loud, hollow chopping sound from Richie's club. "Oooow!" scowled Mr. Kim, "I was trying to surprise you!" She hadn't expected him home for another two days. They looked at each other, collapsing into giggles.

5. In this passage, what **most** likely causes the noise that Mrs. Kim hears coming from the back of the house?

   A. Snickers, the dog, is playing around outside.

   B. Richie is playing golf.

   C. Mr. Kim is sneaking in to surprise her.

   D. Mrs. Kim is having tea.

6. In this passage, what is the effect of Mr. Kim's sneaking up on Mrs. Kim?

   A. Mrs. Kim needs tea and meditation.

   B. Mrs. Kim wears fuzzy slippers.

   C. Richie plays golf with his little play golf club.

   D. Mrs. Kim hits Mr. Kim with Richie's play golf club.

It was Friday evening, and Tonia was excited to have friends over. Just as she slid a tray of chocolate chip cookie dough into the oven to bake, the phone rang. It was Alyssa. "What's up? We can watch *Shrek*. No, it's not just for kids…OK, so when will you be over? Of course I do; don't I always have snacks?" The girls chatted on the phone about their plans for the evening. Before she knew it, they had launched into a conversation about school and gymnastics team gossip. While she was giggling hysterically about something Tim O'Connor had done last week, an alarm went off in Tonia's mind. Sniffing, she thought to herself, "Do I smell something burning?" Oh no! The cookies. "Gotta go," she blurted to Alyssa before rushing back to the kitchen. She opened the oven to a tray of crispy chocolate chip rocks. She had overdone the talking *and* the snacks!

7. In this passage, what causes Tonia to be excited?

   A. She is baking cookies.

   C. She is having friends over.

   B. She is planning to watch *Shrek*.

   D. She hears from Tim O'Connor.

8. In this passage, what causes Tonia to burn the cookies?

   A. She is watching *Shrek,* and she is not paying attention.

   B. She is talking on the telephone, and she is not paying attention.

   C. She is talking to Tim O'Connor and not paying attention.

   D. The oven is new, and she does not know how to operate it properly.

Middle school and high school have some similar qualities, but they are also different in many ways. For one, there is the issue of lockers. Students in both middle and high school have assigned lockers. However, middle school students are sometimes restricted as to how and when to use lockers. High schoolers generally have the choice to use them after every class period. Next, there are class changes. While both middle and high school students have class changes daily, middle schoolers usually do not have as far to travel between classes. High schoolers may have classes that require them to travel from one end of the campus to the other. Last, there is the issue of homeroom. Students have assigned homerooms in both middle and high school. In middle school, homeroom is generally the very first class of the day. This is not the case with high school. Students in high school have homeroom later in the day, and in some cases, not even every day. It is clear that middle and high school have various similarities and differences.

9. The transitions used in this passage show that the purpose of the passage is **most** likely

   A. definition.

   B. comparison.

   C. contrast.

   D. comparison and contrast.

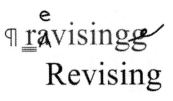

The writing process is the series of steps that good writers use to compose work. The process consists of pre-writing, drafting, revising, and publishing. During each step, writers work toward the successful completion of their work. Each step of the writing process is necessary, as it adds an important element to the final draft of the essay or story. Good writers benefit from adhering to the writing process.

10. The transitions used in this passage show that the purpose of the passage is **most** likely

    A. definition.

    B. comparison.

    C. contrast.

    D. comparison and contrast.

Chapter 4
Reading Persuasive Nonfiction and Multistep Instructions

This chapter addresses the following Georgia Performance Standards for reading:

ELA6LSV2	The student listens to and views various forms of text and media in order to gather and share information, persuade others, and express and understand ideas. The student will select and critically analyze messages using rubrics as assessment tools. When responding to visual and oral texts and media (e.g., television, radio, film productions, and electronic media), the student:
	a. Identifies persuasive and propaganda techniques used in media and identifies false and misleading information.
ELA6R1	The student demonstrates comprehension and shows evidence of a warranted and responsible explanation of a variety of literary and informational texts. For informational texts, the student reads and comprehends in order to develop understanding and expertise and produces evidence of reading that:
	e. Follows multi-step instructions to complete or create a simple product.

This chapter is about reading specific types of informational texts. **Informational texts** are nonfiction literature that conveys facts. Sometimes, through informational texts, readers learn how to carry out and accomplish specific tasks, as in the case of instructions. Other informational literature may focus on persuading or influencing a reader. After reading this chapter, you will be able to recognize the following aspects of informational texts:

- propaganda techniques
- multistep instructions

We will begin with a look at propaganda.

PROPAGANDA TECHNIQUES

In chapter 1, you learned that when writers write, they have specific purposes in mind. You also learned that one goal of writing is to **persuade**. In persuasive writing, writers seek to influence or to change the mind of the reader. While there are many types of persuasive writing, **propaganda** is a form of persuasive writing that is common in politics, advertising, and other areas that involve public opinion.

Propaganda is information, ideas, or rumors spread widely to help or harm a person, movement, organization, nation, or company. Propaganda is used in many forms. Let's take a look at some of the types of propaganda used.

CARD STACKING

Card stacking is a propaganda technique that emphasizes one side of a product or issue. In other words, the writer who uses this propaganda technique "stacks the cards" in favor of one side. Card stacking often downplays other aspects or similar products that are not as positive. In this way, people are influenced to choose one idea or product over the other because it appears to be the best.

Example: When consumers go to purchase cars, they are often bombarded with card-stacking sales pitches. In an effort to separate its product from the competition, for example, a car manufacturer might emphasize all of the positive features of its product. A prospective buyer might be persuaded with comments about the new car, such as the following:

- This car is environmentally friendly.
- This car gets excellent gas mileage.
- This car will look great in your driveway.
- This car will please the whole family.

In the case of card stacking, all of the details presented are slanted in favor of the product.

BANDWAGON

The **bandwagon technique** uses the theory that "everybody is doing it." In this way, writers using bandwagon propaganda influence readers' decisions.

Example: A bandwagon propaganda piece will feature lots of people who are enjoying the product. For example, a bandwagon advertisement for an acne cream might show large numbers of teens using the product with great results. The idea is that prospective consumers feel that they are being left out of the latest trend if they do not also take a part in purchasing the featured product.

TESTIMONIAL

The **testimonial propaganda technique** uses the influence of experts, celebrities, or customers to endorse ideas and products. This technique relies upon the reputation of chosen endorsers to promote a product or program. These endorsers then influence the audience by praising the product or idea being presented.

Nine out of ten dentists recommend FreshPaste to their patients.

> **Example:** When cereal, vitamin, and energy drink companies use athletes to endorse their products, they are using testimonial-style propaganda. The implication is that these people of status have achieved their greatness due, partially at least, to the use of the company's product. Their endorsement of the cereal, vitamin, and/or energy drink gives a testimony to the effectiveness of the featured product.

GLITTERING GENERALITIES

The **glittering generalities technique** uses emotionally appealing words to promote a product or idea. No concrete argument is ever presented. Rather, the audience is charmed by the attractive and influential words of the writer.

> **Example:** An example of the glittering generalities propaganda technique would be a commercial for a vacation package that appeals to the emotions of the consumer. The vacation advertisement might make statements such as these:
>
> - Lose yourself in paradise.
> - Leave the troubles of your life behind.
> - Find your happiness.

All of these statements might seem very tempting to someone who is looking for a vacation. However, none of the statements offer any sound facts or details about the vacation package or the destination.

REPETITION

The **repetition** technique uses a word, jingle, or catch phrase over and over. This phrase is so catchy that it sticks with the reader or audience. It is repeated over and over again.

Example: A shoe store might use a jingle, such as, "At Fleet Feet, we love your feet, and our prices can't be beat. We're Fleet Feet, and we love your feet!" While this is a simple rhyme, it is catchy and, set to music, could stick with a consumer.

TRANSFER

This technique is also called **association**. Like the testimonial technique, **transfer** often uses celebrity endorsers. This propaganda seeks to persuade the reader to use a product or embrace an ideal. In doing so, the reader will receive the same benefits as did the endorser. The idea is that the qualities will transfer to the consumer by use of the product being advertised.

Example: An example of the transfer technique would be an advertisement that shows a beautiful lady who is advertising a beauty skin cream. Prospective consumers might be influenced by her beauty to believe that they, too, can be so beautiful by use of the beauty cream product she sells.

Practice 1: Propaganda

Identify the propaganda technique used in each passage.

card stacking	bandwagon	testimonial
glittering generalities	repetition	transfer

The makers of the Kruiser Yorker are practical patriots who are just like you. The Kruiser Yorker is a new car that is the best in its class of hybrid compact vehicles. It is an American made vehicle that is just perfect for everything. From getting baby safely around town, to getting your college student to and from campus, the Kruiser Yorker is the practical choice for patriots all over the country. Also, with the benefit of the hybrid features, the Kruiser Yorker is the perfect choice for the environment. Why buy anywhere else? Come on down to your local Kruiser Yorker dealer today. Our flags are raised. We are waiting for you.

1. What propagnda technique is used **most** in this passage?

    A. transfer   **B.** testimonial   **C.** card stacking   **D.** glittering generalities

The Helen Jiles waffle maker is the choice of old-fashioned cooks everywhere. Unlike many of your run-of-the mill waffle makers, the HJ unit is handmade of the finest materials. This makes for old-fashioned, down-home cooking, and the tastiest waffles around. Why spend more money for all of those fancy big name brands? The HJ waffle maker is manufactured by the small Jiles family that has been in the waffle industry going back into the 1800s. Plus, those other waffle maker companies cannot offer you the personal service that the HJ company can. We will deliver the waffle maker right to your door complete with the family recipe for the best waffle selections you will ever taste. Call to place your order with us today.

2. What propaganda technique is used **most** in this passage?

    A. repetition   **B.** bandwagon   **C.** card stacking   **D.** glittering generalities

The last time you made family vacation plans, did you do it yourself? Well, there is no longer a need for that. Besides, who has the time? With the hustle and bustle of day-to-day, why make your own travel arrangements? Leave it to the Vacation Vigilantes. We are an independent agency that will work to meet your personal needs. In fact, if you asked a handful of people you know, you're bound to find that four out of five of them have already tried and loved our services. In fact, young, beautiful pop sensation singer, Tiffany Hall is one of our valued customers. Tiffany has to travel all over the world. She just hasn't the time to sit on the phone or computer trying to find the best rates and arrangements. However, we do. After using Vacation Vigilantes, Tiffany is now carefree. You, too, can be as carefree as popular young singer, Tiffany, when it comes to travel plans; just try our services, and you will see. Hey, if Tiffany, and just about everyone one else you know trusts getaway plans to the Vacation Vigilantes, why won't you? Give us a call today.

3. What propaganda technique is used **most** in this passage?

    A. transfer   **B.** repetition   **C.** bandwagon   **D.** card stacking

4. What sort of propaganda technique uses the faces and statements of popular sports athletes to sell cereal, energy drinks, and training products?

    A. repetition   **B.** testimonial   **C.** bandwagon   **D.** glittering generalities

UNDERSTANDING MULTISTEP INSTRUCTIONS

Have you ever visited a bookstore and noticed all of the "how-to" books there are? There are recipe books that tell you how to cook, crafting books that tell you how to create arts and crafts, art books that tell you how to draw, and so on. Reading informational literature is a good way for people to learn how to do many things. Often, "how-to" books present steps for a reader to follow. These steps are presented in a 1-2-3, or **chronological**, order that makes it easy for the reader to follow and understand. Because instructions have several or sometimes many steps, they are called **multistep instructions**.

    Example: Read the following multistep directions on *How to Ride a Bike*. Notice that each step goes in the order that it should happen.

How to Ride a Bike

First, you should dress properly. Wear a helmet and elbow/knee pads for your best protection. Then, go out to a safe area. Be sure to bring along an adult who will be able to help you. Next, get on the bike, and try to find your balance with the adult helper holding the back of your bike. Finally, begin to pedal, allowing the adult to help keep you steady until you are able to balance on your own.

Practice 2: Understanding Instructions

Directions: Read the instructions and answer the questions that follow.

How to Make Chocolate Chip Cookies

Ingredients:

- 2 1/4 cups all-purpose flour
- 1 teaspoon baking soda
- 1 teaspoon salt
- 1 cup (2 sticks) butter, softened
- 3/4 cup granulated sugar
- 3/4 cup packed brown sugar
- 1 teaspoon vanilla extract
- 2 large eggs
- 2 cups (12-oz. pkg.) Semi-Sweet Chocolate Morsels
- 1 cup chopped nuts
- Small bowl

Directions

1. Gather your cooking ingredients.

2. Preheat the oven to 375° F.

3. Combine the flour, baking soda, and salt in a small bowl.

4. Beat butter, granulated sugar, brown sugar, and vanilla extract in a large mixer bowl until creamy. Add eggs, one at a time, beating well after each addition.

5. Gradually beat flour mixture into the butter mixture.

6. Stir in morsels and nuts.

7. Drop by rounded tablespoons onto an ungreased baking sheet.

8. Bake for 9 to 11 minutes or until golden brown.

9. Cool on baking sheets for two minutes.

10. Remove to wire racks to cool completely.

---

1. What do these multistep instructions teach a reader how to do?

   A. make chocolate   C. combine ingredients

   B. make nut bars   D. make chocolate chip cookies

2. During which step are the cookies finished baking?

   A. step 6   B. step 8   C. step 9   D. step 10

3. During which step should you add the nuts?

   A. step 3   B. step 4   C. step 5   D. step 6

4. What should you do before you preheat the oven?

   A. gather cooking ingredients   C. preheat the cooking ingredients

   B. remove the oven's wire racks   D. stir in morsels and nuts

5. Do you combine the flour, baking soda, and salt before or after making the butter mixture?

   A. before   B. after

CHAPTER 4 SUMMARY

Propaganda is a form of persuasive writing. Propaganda is information, ideas, or rumors spread widely to help or harm a person, movement, organization, nation, or company.

> **Card stacking** is a propaganda technique that emphasizes one side of a product or issue. Card stacking often downplays the benefit of the other side or product being advertised.

> The **bandwagon** technique uses the theory that "everybody is doing it."

> **Testimonials** use the influence of experts, celebrities, or customers to endorse ideas and products.

> The **glittering generalities** technique uses emotionally appealing words to promote a product or idea. No concrete argument is ever presented.

> **Repetition** uses a jingle or catch phrase over and over again. This phrase is so catchy that it sticks with the reader or audience. It is repeated over and over again.

> **Transfer**, like the testimonial technique, often uses celebrity endorsers. This propaganda seeks to persuade the reader to use a product or embrace an ideal. In doing so, the reader will receive the same benefits as did the celebrity endorser.

Understanding **multistep instructions** will help you learn from directions, articles, and books designed to teach you how to do something. The multiple steps (that's why they're called multistep instructions) are presented in a 1-2-3, or chronological, order that makes it easy for you to understand.

CHAPTER 4 REVIEW

Read each passage and choose the propaganda technique that is being used.

Buy Junco paper windmills today. Made of the finest quality paper, these lightweight toys provide hours of entertainment for the imaginative child. They are affordable and educational. What are you waiting for?

1.   **A.** bandwagon   **C.** card stacking

       B. testimonial   **D.** glittering generalities

Pretty Lips lip gloss is better than the rest. It comes in ten fruity flavors and is priced below the competitor's product. Unlike those other glosses that are hard to find, Pretty Lips is available at a store near you.

2.   **A.** bandwagon   **C.** card stacking

       B. testimonial   **D.** repetition

Everybody is shopping at Jones' Jean Junction. We have the best prices on used jeans of every variety. Don't be left out. Get down to the junction to purchase your pair today.

3.   **A.** bandwagon   **C.** card stacking

       B. transfer   **D.** glittering generalities

Greedy Grapes gum is your yummy choice for long lasting bubble gum flavor. Greedy Grapes is fun to chew. Your friends will wonder about your fruity smell and purple mouth. Greedy, greedy, greedy, they'll call you as you gobble wads of Greedy Grapes.

4.   **A.** bandwagon   **C.** glittering generalities

       B. transfer   **D.** repetition

Take it from me, Sue Thomas, gold medalist figure skater, Hartson's muscle rub is the best choice after a long, hard workout on the ice.

5.   **A.** association   **C.** testimonial

       B. transfer   **D.** bandwagon

Read the multistep directions for making pumpkin pie. Answer the questions that follow.

INGREDIENTS

- 1 medium sugar pumpkin
- 1 tablespoon vegetable oil
- 1 recipe pastry for a 9 inch single crust pie
- 1/2 teaspoon ground ginger
- 1/2 teaspoon ground cinnamon
- 1 teaspoon salt
- 4 eggs, lightly beaten
- 1 cup honey, warmed slightly
- 1/2 cup milk
- 1/2 cup heavy whipping cream

1. Gather your ingredients.
2. Preheat the oven to 325 degrees F (165 degrees C).
3. Cut pumpkin in half, and remove seeds.
4. Lightly oil the cut surface of the pumpkin.
5. Place cut side down on a jelly roll pan lined with foil and lightly oiled. Bake at 325 degrees F (165 degrees C) until the flesh is tender when poked with a fork. Cool until just warm. Scrape the pumpkin flesh from the peel. Either mash, or puree in small batches in a blender.
6. In large bowl, blend together 2 cups pumpkin puree, spices, and salt. Beat in eggs, honey, milk, and cream. Pour filling into pie shell.
7. Bake at 400 degrees F (205 degrees C) for 50 to 55 minutes, or until a knife inserted 1 inch from edge of pie comes out clean. When it is done, remove it from the oven.
8. Cool on a wire rack.

6. What should you do first?

    A. oil the pumpkin

    B. gather your ingredients

    C. blend the ingredients

    D. cool the pumpkin

7. What should you do last?

    A. oil the pumpkin

    B. gather your ingredients

    C. blend the ingredients

    D. cool the pie on a wire rack

8. When should you oil the pumpkin?

    A. never

    B. before it is cut

    C. after it is cut

    D. whenever you want

9. During which step should you preheat the oven?

    A. step 1

    B. step 2

    C. step 3

    D. step 4

10. During which step should the pumpkin pie be removed from the oven?

    A. step 5

    B. step 6

    C. step 7

    D. step 8

Chapter 5
Graphics and Organization in Informational Texts

This chapter addresses the following Georgia Performance Standards for reading:

ELA6R1	The student demonstrates comprehension and shows evidence of a warranted and responsible explanation of a variety of literary and informational texts.
	For literary texts, the student identifies the characteristics of various genres and produces evidence of reading that:
	b. Applies knowledge of common graphic features (i.e., graphic organizers, diagrams, captions, illustrations, charts, tables, graphs).
ELA6RC2	The student participates in discussions related to curricular learning in all subject areas. The student:
	d. Evaluates the merits of texts in every subject discipline.

In this chapter, you will improve your skills as a reader of informational texts. You will learn to recognize features of informational texts that writers use to help the reader. These include features like glossaries and indices as well as graphics like photographs and charts. You will also learn about organizing informational texts using graphic organizers. Finally, you will learn to evaluate how well all of these features are used to help a reader understand text.

COMMON FEATURES OF INFORMATIONAL TEXTS

Imagine that you are planning a cross-country road trip. What would be one of the most important items to bring along? Did you say a map? Without the map to guide you, how would you know which way to travel? Think about how much time you would waste trying to find your way without the directions that a map provides.

Just as maps guide travelers on trips, writers of informational texts offer tools that help to guide readers through their writing. Two specific tools writers use are **glossaries** and **indices**. Let's take a look at these techniques.

GLOSSARIES

Glossaries are lists of terms and definitions in a special subject. Glossaries are usually located at the back of a book and contain words that are important in the book. Like a dictionary, the words of a glossary are arranged in alphabetical order. Using a glossary while reading nonfiction makes the reading much easier. Take a look at your science, history, and social studies textbooks. Do these books contain glossaries? Can you locate key words in the glossaries that are important to what you have studied in class this year?

INDICES

The word indices is the plural form of the word **index**. An index is an alphabetical listing of names, places, topics, and their page numbers in a book. Indices in books are so important because they allow readers to quickly look up pages that contain the information they need. Without an index, a reader could spend hours searching through a large nonfiction text to find specific topics mentioned on multiple pages. Items in an index are arranged in alphabetical order. This helps the reader to locate the words.

Practice 1: Glossaries and Indices

1. In a glossary, which of the following words would occur first?

    A. atom   **B.** anatomy   **C.** atmosphere   **D.** aerospace

2. Which of the following texts would be **most likely** to contain a glossary?

    A. atlas   **B.** encyclopedia   **C.** textbook   **D.** novel

3. Look at the sample index portion below. Where would a reader find information about author's purpose?

Aesop	148, 149
afix	28, 29
analogy	39, 127
antonym	26, 36, 39
author	
argument	79
logic	58
mood	74
purpose	57, 166, 184

    A. 148, and 149   **C.** 26, 36, and 39

    B. 39 and 127   **D.** 57, 166, and 184

4. Look at the sample index portion below. Which of the following pages does **not** contain information about theme?

tall tale	146
text	
context	184
extended meaning	183
literal meaning	184
theme	144, 173
themes and messages across subject areas	172

A. 144   **B.** 146   **C.** 172   **D.** 173

GRAPHICS

In addition to glossaries and indices, writers of informational texts use **graphics** to assist readers. Graphics are visual representations that help readers to picture and understand what the writer presents. Common examples are the following:

- Graphic Organizers
- Illustrations and Captions
- Diagrams and Graphs
- Charts and Tables

Let's take a look at each feature.

GRAPHIC ORGANIZERS

Graphic organizers provide readers with a visual explanation of ideas. They are charts or pictures that present information in a clear and organized manner. You are probably familiar with some forms of graphic organizers, such as Venn Diagrams and spider maps. Perhaps you have even used them in your own work. Take a look at the following **brainstorm map**. This example is used to identify ideas for great places to vacation.

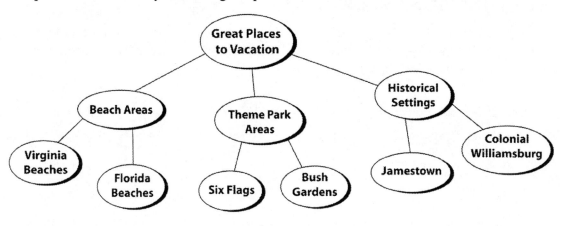

As you can see, this brainstorm map would be a very effective tool for a writer who is planning to write about various vacation places. The key to a good graphic organizer is for information to be presented in a clear and concise manner. Visual ease is important. A reader can quickly look at the map and identify major and minor ideas that the writer is planning.

In addition to using mapping, writers of informational texts sometimes use **Venn Diagrams** as graphic organizers. Venn Diagrams use circles and regions created by overlapping circles to organize information. Look at the following example of a Venn Diagram used to organize the names of students in Mr. Houston's sixth grade class. In this diagram, students are organized into two groups: students who have pets and students who live in apartments. In some cases, students have pets and live in apartments. These students fall in the middle of the diagram. Some students do not have pets or live in apartments. These students fall outside of the diagram. How else do you think a Venn Diagram might be useful in informational texts?

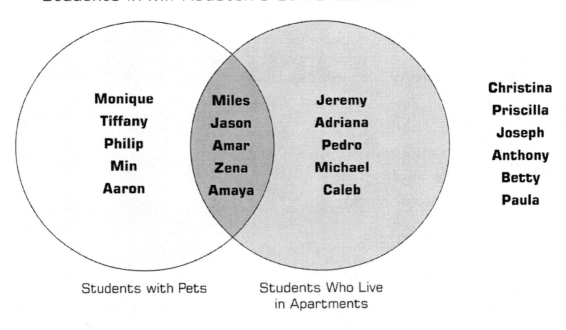

Students in Mr. Houston's 6th Grade Class

Monique	Miles	Jeremy	Christina
Tiffany	Jason	Adriana	Priscilla
Philip	Amar	Pedro	Joseph
Min	Zena	Michael	Anthony
Aaron	Amaya	Caleb	Betty
			Paula

Students with Pets   Students Who Live in Apartments

ILLUSTRATIONS AND CAPTIONS

Illustrations are the pictures used in a text. They may give images of what the writing describes or help to stir the reader's imagination. **Captions** are brief statements underneath illustrations. They explain what is featured in the picture.

ACTIVITY 1: GRAPHICS

Read the passage. After reading, sketch a picture to illustrate the story. Also, write a caption of one or two lines that would accompany your illustration.

"The Wind and the Sun" by Aesop

The Wind and the Sun were disputing which was the stronger. Suddenly they saw a traveler coming down the road, and the Sun said: "I see a way to decide our dispute. Whichever of us can cause that traveler to take off his cloak shall be regarded as the stronger. You begin." So the Sun retired behind a cloud, and the Wind began to blow as hard as it could upon the traveler. But the harder he blew the more closely did the traveler wrap his cloak round him, till at last the Wind had to give up in despair. Then the Sun came out and shone in all his glory upon the traveler, who soon found it too hot to walk with his cloak on.

Kindness has greater effect than severity.

Practice 2:   Illustrations and Captions

Read the following descriptions of pictures. Answer the questions that follow.

1. Which picture would **most** effectively illustrate the passage above?

   A. a picture of the sun hiding behind a cloud

   B. a picture of the wind blowing hard on a traveler

   C. a picture of the traveler who is suffering from heat

   D. a picture of a traveler with a sun and the wind talking behind him

2. Which caption would **most likely** accompany the illustration of the above passage?

   A. A traveler passes on a lonely road.

   B. The sun hides behind a cloud, waiting for a traveler on the road.

   C. The wind and sun see the traveler as a way to settle their dispute.

   D. A traveler is too hot from the rays of the sun.

DIAGRAMS AND GRAPHS

A **diagram** is a very detailed illustration. It often uses labels to identify specific parts of the pictured item. For example, a science book might use a diagram to show the earth's layers.

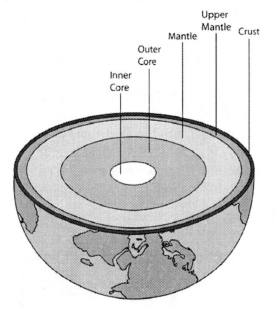

One type of diagram is a **graph**. A graph is a diagram used to present data. There are many types of graphs. Some common types are **bar graphs**, **line graphs**, and **pie charts**.

Birthday Gifts Received by Mrs. Hill's 6th Grade Class

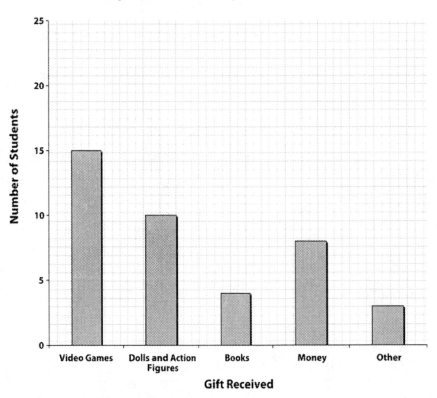

ACTIVITY 2: MORE GRAPHICS

Draw a diagram of your classroom. Include important features such as the door, windows, shelves, teacher's desk, student desks, class library, etc.

Practice 3: Diagrams and Graphs

Use the graph provided to answer the questions that follow.

Ice Cream Favorites of Sugar Creek Middle School Students

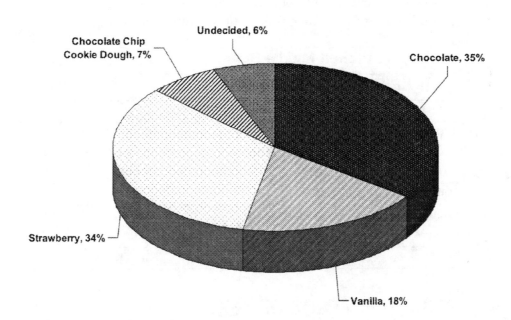

1. What percentage of students has decided upon a favorite ice cream flavor?

    A. 6%   **C.** 94%

    B. 50%   **D.** not enough information provided

2. What is the difference in the percentage of students who prefer vanilla and those who like chocolate chip cookie dough?

    A. 15%   **B.** 11%   **C.** 1%   **D.** 12%

3. What is the combined percentage of students who prefer chocolate and strawberry ice cream?

    A. 69%   **B.** 94%   **C.** 100%   **D.** none of these

4. Which ice cream flavor is **most** preferred among the students?

   A. chocolate

   B. vanilla

   C. strawberry

   D. chocolate chip cookie dough

5. Which ice cream flavor is **least** preferred among the students?

   A. chocolate

   B. vanilla

   C. strawberry

   D. chocolate chip cookie dough

CHARTS AND TABLES

Charts give reader information in an organized, easy-to-follow format. A **table** is a type of chart that uses columns and rows to organize information for the reader.

Pritchett Middle School Class Schedule		
PERIOD	**TIME**	**SUBJECT**
Homeroom	8:15–8:30	
Period I	8:35–9:30	Language Arts
Period II	9:40–11:00	Related Arts (P.E., Health, Art, etc.)
Period III	11:15–12:10	Lunch
Period IV	12:15–1:10	Math
Period V	1:15–2:10	Science
Period VI	2:15–3:10	Social Studies

EVALUATING THE MERITS OF TEXT

An important aspect of reading informational texts is being able to decide when what you are reading is well written and accomplishes its goal. For example, if you are reading a passage from your language arts textbook that explains how to go through the writing process, when you have finished reading, you should understand the writing process. The writing should have the **merits** (qualities) of being clear, informative, and well explained, so that you are able to gain knowledge of what the writer presented to you. The following areas are important features to consider about a text that you are evaluating:

- **Language:** Language refers to the writer's choice of words.
- **Content:** Content is what the writer has chosen to include to inform you, the reader.
- **Organization:** Organization refers to the writer's way of arranging ideas so that they are most effectively communicated to and understood by the reader.
- **Reader:** You are the reader. It is up to you do determine how effectively the text has been written.

Take a look at the following table. This table features some strong tips on how to evaluate the merits of a text you are reading.

Questions for Evaluating the Merits of Text	
Language	Is the writing clear? Is the language understandable? Does the writer define very difficult words?
Content	Are main ideas well supported? Are important ideas explained? Do the supporting details better explain main ideas?
Organization	Is the writing well organized?
Reader	Does the reader gain the intended knowledge?

Practice 4: Tables, Charts, and Evaluating the Merits of Text

Use the table provided above to answer the questions that follow.

1. Which of the following questions **most** involves the reader's response?

   A. Are important ideas explained?

   B. Are main ideas well supported?

   C. Is the writing well organized?

   D. Does the reader gain the intended knowledge?

2. Which of the following questions does **not** involve content?

   A. Are main ideas well supported?

   B. Are important ideas explained?

   C. Do the supporting details better explain main ideas?

   D. Is the writing well organized?

3. Which of the following questions would **not** help to clarify the language of the text?

   A. Are the main ideas well supported?

   B. Is the writing clear?

   C. Is the language understandable?

   D. Does the writer define very difficult words?

Read the passage with attention to evaluating its merits.

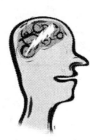

When a writer sits down to write, the first thing that he/she should do is to consider the writing topic through brainstorming. In the brainstorming phase of the writing process, the objective is to generate ideas. There are many ways to accomplish this task, and it is up to the writer to decide which brainstorming method is most effective for him/her. One method of brainstorming is **webbing**. Webbing is a technique in which a writer begins with a central idea, and branches out with smaller, but related ideas. The writer uses a graphic organizer that looks like a web to help organize ideas. Another method of brainstorming is **free writing**. In the process of free writing, a writer simply begins to write, without worrying about grammatical rules or spelling. The objective is to generate ideas by writing as much as possible, as quickly as possible. A third method of brainstorming is **journaling**. Journaling is a technique that writers might do over time. A writer who journals as a way of brainstorming would keep an ongoing log of ideas in a notebook, or journal. Whenever ideas occur to the writer, he/she would jot them in a journal to save for later use. As there are so many methods of brainstorming, every writer can find a method that works. It is important not to skip this step of the writing process, as brainstorming allows a writer to come up with the best and most creative ideas possible.

4. Now that you have read the passage, discuss with a partner how well the writer accomplished the intended purpose of informing the reader on the brainstorming step of the writing process. Consider these domains: language, content, organization, reader response. How could the writer have more effectively presented this information?

CHAPTER 5 SUMMARY

Glossaries are lists of terms and definitions in a special subject. Glossaries are usually located at the back of a book and contain words that are important in the book.

The word **indices** is the plural form of the word index. Indices are alphabetical listings of names, places, topics, and their page number locations in a book. Indices in books are so important because they allow readers to be able to quickly locate pages that contain desired information.

Illustrations are the pictures used in a text. They may give images of what the writing describes or help to stir the reader's imagination. **Captions** are brief statements underneath illustrations. They explain what is featured in the picture.

A **diagram** is a very detailed illustration. It often uses labels to identify specific parts of the pictured item. For example, a science book might use a diagram to show the earth's layers. One type of diagram is a **graph**. A graph is a diagram used to present data.

Charts give readers information in a very organized, easy-to-follow format. The **table** is a type of chart that uses columns and rows to organize information for the reader.

Graphic organizers are visual tools that writers use to help readers better understand the ideas presented in informational texts. There are many types of graphic organizers. Examples are Venn diagrams and spider maps.

Evaluating the Merits of Text

An important aspect of reading informational texts is being able to decide when what you are reading is well written and accomplishes the task of the writer. This is called **evaluating the merits of a text**. The following areas are important features to consider about a text that you are evaluating:

- **Language:** Language refers to the writer's choice of words.
- **Content:** Content is what the writer has chosen to write to inform you, the reader.
- **Organization:** Organization refers to the writer's way of arranging details so that they are most effectively communicated to and understood by the reader.
- **Reader:** You are the reader. It is up to you do determine how effectively the text has been written.

CHAPTER 5 REVIEW

1. In a glossary, which entry would occur last?

   A. biosphere   **B.** biodegradable   **C.** biology   **D.** biogenetics

2. In a glossary, which entry would occur first?

   A. biosphere   **B.** biodegradable   **C.** biology   **D.** biogenetics

Virginia Colony	
founding	28, 29
government	39, 127
hardships	
enemies	79
financial backing	58
starvation	17

3. According to the index, on what page would a reader find information about starvation in the Virginia colony?

   A. 26 and 36   **B.** 39   **C.** 17   **D.** 74

4. According to the index, on which page would a reader find information about the colony's government?

   A. 28   **B.** 39 and 127   **C.** 26, 36, and 39   **D.** 74

5. According to the index, on which page would a reader find information about hardships?

   A. 79   **C.** 17

   B. 58   **D.** all of the above

Read the passage, and then answer the question that follows.

The Fox and the Stork
by Aesop

At one time, the Fox and the Stork were on visiting terms and seemed very good friends. So the Fox invited the Stork to dinner, and for a joke put nothing before her but some soup in a very shallow dish. This the Fox could easily lap up, but the Stork could only wet the end of her long bill in it, and left the meal as hungry as when she began. "I am sorry," said the Fox, "the soup is not to your liking."

"Pray do not apologize," said the Stork. "I hope you will return this visit, and come and dine with me soon." So a day was appointed when the Fox should visit the Stork; but when they were seated at table all that was for their dinner was contained in a very long-necked jar with a narrow mouth, in which the Fox could not insert his snout, so all he could manage to do was to lick the outside of the jar.

"I will not apologize for the dinner," said the Stork.

"One bad turn deserves another."

6. Which illustration would be **most** appropriate?

    A. a picture of soup set on a dinner table

    B. a picture of a fox trying to lap from a narrow mouth jar

    C. a picture of a stork trying to sip from a shallow dish

    D. a combination of B and C

Use the graph provided to answer the questions that follow.

Favorite Colors of Students at Washington Middle School

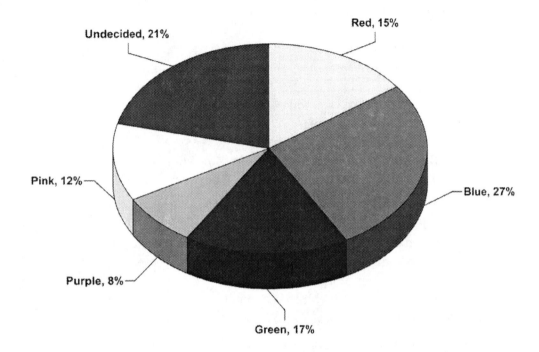

7. What is the percentage of students that has not decided about a color?

   A. 21%   **B.** 79%   **C.** 15%   **D.** 27%

8. What is the difference between the percentage of students preferring green and pink?

   A. 17%   **B.** 12%   **C.** 5%   **D.** 29%

Use the graphics provided to answer the question that follows.

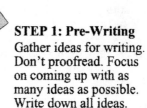

STEP 1: Pre-Writing
Gather ideas for writing. Don't proofread. Focus on coming up with as many ideas as possible. Write down all ideas.

STEP 4: Proofreading
Make a final check for errors in your revised essay. Present your essay for class.

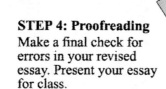

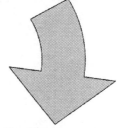

STEP 2: Drafting
Write the first version of your work. Use only the pre-writing ideas that fit into your paper.

STEP 3: Revision
Go over your draft to eliminate errors. Look for problems with content, organization, grammar, and writing style. Re-write your draft.

	Process	Guidelines
STEP 1	Pre-Writing	Gather ideas for writing. Don't proofread. Focus on coming up with as many ideas as possible. Write down all ideas.
STEP 2	Drafting	Write the first version of your work. Use only the pre-writing ideas that fit into your paper.
STEP 3	Revision	Go over your draft to eliminate errors. Look for problems with content, organization, grammar, and writing style. Re-write your draft.
STEP 4	Proofreading and Publishing	Make a final check for errors in your revised essay. Present your essay for class.

9. During which step does the writer **not** have to consider spelling?

    A. proofreading and publishing   **C.** drafting

    B. pre-writing   **D.** revision

10. During which step is the finished paper ready to be turned in?

    A. proofreading and publishing   **C.** drafting

    B. pre-writing   **D.** revision

11. During which step should a writer correct major errors?

    A. pre-writing

    B. drafting

    C. revision

    D. proofreading and publishing

12. During which step should a writer correct minor errors?

    A. pre-writing

    B. drafting

    C. revision

    D. proofreading and publishing

Chapter 6
Sensory Details and Figurative Language

This chapter addresses the following Georgia Performance Standards for reading:

ELA6R1	The student demonstrates comprehension and shows evidence of a warranted and responsible explanation of a variety of literary and informational texts.
	a. Identifies and analyzes sensory details and figurative language.
	h. Responds to and explains the effects of sound, figurative language, and graphics in order to uncover the meaning in literature:
	i. Sound (e.g., alliteration, onomatopoeia, rhyme scheme)
	ii. Figurative language (i.e., simile, metaphor, hyperbole, personification)

Have you ever read a book that did not have pictures? As you read, were you able to form pictures in your mind about the scenes in the book? One goal that good writers have is to captivate and hold the interest of the reader. To do this, they often create humorous and exciting plot lines. Another way that writers help readers to tune in is to use colorful language. This language interests the reader while offering creative ways for a reader to understand the writing.

In this chapter, you will look at several forms of **sensory detail** and **figurative language**. You will learn to recognize these techniques in the stories and poetry that you read.

FIGURATIVE LANGUAGE

Writers have the creative freedom to use words in many ways. Often, it is the way in which a writer uses words that makes a text interesting to the reader. Many writers use **figurative language** as a colorful way to express themselves. Figurative language, which is a non-literal or otherwise creative use of words, comes in many forms. In some cases, a writer uses expressions that a reader can visualize. This helps a reader to better understand a writer's intent. Also, figurative language may come in the form of sound devices that add humor, charm, rhythm, or emphasis to a work. Here are some examples:

"I am so hungry I could eat a cow."

This phrase offers a funny image. A person eating a cow would be a tremendous feat. However, it simply means that the person who says such a thing is very hungry.

"We're all swimming in the sea of life."

Life is not actually a sea. However, comparing life to a sea helps to impart an image that a reader could imagine.

"Charlie's little brother eats like a pig."

You could imagine a boy who eats in a greedy and very sloppy manner.

IDIOMS

One form of figurative language is the use of **idioms**. An idiom is an expression using words that are not meant to be taken literally. It contains words that people commonly know. But the words are used in an uncommon way. For example, *raining cats and dogs*, *cat nap*, and *cat's got your tongue*, are all examples of idioms. When people say it is raining cats and dogs, they do not mean that cats and dogs are falling from the sky like rain. Rather, this means that it is raining very hard. Taking a cat nap means to take a short nap. When someone asks if a cat's got your tongue, it means that you are not speaking much or at all. As you will notice, all of these expressions use common words. Yet, their meanings do not match with the words used. Writers use idioms in fiction and poetry. People also use idioms in everyday conversation.

Here are some other examples of commonly used idiomatic expressions and their meanings:

Idiom	Literal Meaning
"diamond in the rough"	someone/something has great untapped potential
"walking on eggshells"	a very unstable/insecure situation
"baker's dozen"	a set of thirteen
"blind leading the blind"	an inexperienced pair or group
"chip on his/her shoulder"	a person who carries a grudge
"to go out on a limb"	to take a chance
"have an axe to grind"	someone who is seeking revenge
"wash my hands of it"	to stop being involved in a situation
"know the ropes"	to have experience
"mum's the word."	a vow to secrecy

Practice 1:   Idioms

Read each of the following sentences. Choose the letter that identifies the meaning of the underlined idiom. Use context clues to help you.

1. After the last day of the school year, Amanda skipped home, <u>as free as a bird</u>. In the sentence, "as free as a bird" means that

    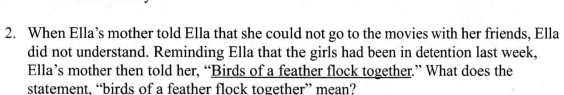

    A. Amanda thinks birds should be free.

    B. Amanda is carefree and unburdened.

    C. Amanda enjoys birds.

    D. Amanda can fly.

2. When Ella's mother told Ella that she could not go to the movies with her friends, Ella did not understand. Reminding Ella that the girls had been in detention last week, Ella's mother then told her, "<u>Birds of a feather flock together</u>." What does the statement, "birds of a feather flock together" mean?

    A. It means that Ella's mother is a birdwatcher and likes to see whole flocks of birds flying together.

    B. It means that Ella likes birds very much.

    C. It means that Ella's mother thinks Ella will become like the people with whom she associates.

    D. none of the above

3. When Chauncy refused to go up the hill to the old haunted house, his friends said he was <u>chicken-livered</u>. The expression "chicken-livered" means

    A. elegant.   **B.** fearless.   **C.** angry.   **D.** cowardly.

4. When Mrs. Wilson told the class a spooky ghost story, the class was <u>all ears</u>. The expression "all ears" means

    A. listening intently.   **C.** having lots of ears.

    B. hardly listening.   **D.** none of the above.

5. Darla is <u>the apple of her mother's eye</u>. The phrase "apple of her eye" means that

    A. Darla's mother has an apple in her eye.

    B. Darla's mother adores her daughter, Darla.

    C. Darla's eyes are as red as apples from crying to her mom.

    D. Darla's mother had the reflection of an apple in her eye.

METAPHOR

Another form of figurative language is the **metaphor**. Writers often use metaphors for emphasis or explanation. A metaphor is a comparison of two things that are not otherwise alike. An example of a metaphor would be: *His eyes were huge saucers, spinning in every direction.* Of course, no one has eyes that are saucers, but when a writer uses an image such as a saucer, a reader immediately has a picture in mind of big, wide eyes, looking in all directions.

Another example of a metaphor would be: *After she ran the race, Amy's legs were limp spaghetti beneath her.* What could it mean for someone to be described as having "spaghetti legs"?

In the first example, a character's eyes are being compared to huge saucers. Perhaps, his eyes are large or wide as he looked around, maybe in surprise or fear.

In the next example, Amy's legs are compared to limp spaghetti. Her legs are weak and limp (like cooked spaghetti) from running for so long. Again, spaghetti is nothing like legs. This comparison lets a reader know right away how weak Amy's legs felt.

Practice 2: Identifying Metaphors

1. Which of the following sentences contains a metaphor?

   A. He is a pig.

   B. He eats a lot.

   C. He is very hungry.

   D. He likes pigs.

2. Which of the following sentences contains a metaphor?

   A. You make me happy.

   B. The sunshine makes me happy.

   C. Your smile is like sunshine.

   D. You are the sunshine of my life.

3. Disgusted, Maren's mother looked around at her daughter's <u>pigsty of a room</u>. The use of the expression "pigsty of a room" means that

   A. Maren's room is an actual pigsty.

   B. Maren has pigs in her room

   C. Maren's room is as messy as a pigsty.

   D. Maren's mother doesn't like pigs.

4. The man greeted his former playground bully with <u>an icy stare.</u> "An icy stare" means

A. a cold day outside.

C. a look that mimics ice.

B. an angry look.

D. none of the above.

SIMILE

Like a metaphor, a **simile** is a comparison of two things. However, a metaphor is a direct comparison, whereas a simile uses *like* or *as* to compare. Here are two examples of similes:

> **Example:** Mary slept like a baby.

> **Example:** Chad was as tall as a giraffe.

In the first example, the character Mary slept so restfully, it was similar to the sleep of a baby. In the second example, Chad is so tall, it reminds one of a giraffe. The words *like* and *as* are used to make the comparisons.

Practice 3: Identifying Similes

Identify the meaning of the underlined simile in each sentence.

> After a warm bath and a cup of tea, Eunice <u>slept like a baby</u>.

1. How does the expression "slept like a baby" affect the meaning of this sentence?

A. Eunice slept soundly and peacefully.

B. Eunice tossed and turned throughout the night.

C. Eunice looked very young and small when she slept.

D. none of these

> When Anna's mother saw that her daughter was taking a break from her chores, she scolded her. "Don't just sit there <u>like a bump on a log</u>," her mother said, annoyed.

2. How does the expression "like a bump on a log" affect the meaning of this sentence?

A. Anna's mother is annoyed by logs.

B. Anna's mother is annoyed when her daughter sits on a log.

C. Anna's mother is annoyed to see her daughter doing nothing.

D. none of these

The girls sat wide-eyed, <u>as quiet as church mice</u>.

3. "As quiet as church mice" means that

    A. the girls were extremely noisy.

    B. the girls made the noises of mice.

    C. the girls were very quiet.

    D. none of the above

Without her glasses, she was <u>as blind as a bat</u>.

4. "As blind as a bat" means that

    A. she has eyes like a bat.   **C.** the girl acts like a bat.

    B. the girl cannot see well.   **D.** none of the above

When Marla removed her gloves, her hands were <u>like ice</u>

5. "Like ice" means that

    A. Marla's hands were icy cold.   **C.** Marla had ice on her hands.

    B. Marla likes ice.   **D.** none of the above

Aditya was <u>as busy as a beaver</u>.

6. "As busy as a beaver" means

    A. working all the time.   **C.** that Aditya likes beavers.

    B. quite lazy.   **D.** none of the above

Harriet gave up; talking to her brother was <u>like talking to a brick wall</u>.

7. "Like talking to a brick wall" means that

    A. Harriet and her brother talk near a brick wall.

    B. Harriet's brother feels that talking to Harriet is useless.

    C. Harriet and her brother spend time talking to brick walls.

    D. none of these

Doug's big dog is <u>as gentle as a lamb</u>.

8. "As gentle as a lamb" means that

    A. the dog looks like a lamb.   **C.** the dog is mean.

    B. the dog is very affectionate.   **D.** none of the above

HYPERBOLE

Hyperbole (high-**pur**-buh-lee) is exaggeration used for emphasis. It is also known as overstatement. Hyperbole statements are not literally true. They help the writer or speaker emphasize a point. For example, when someone says, "I've told you a thousand times already," this is a hyperbole. Have they really told you something a thousand times? They probably have not. This means, however, that they have said something too many times to count. Can you think of hyperboles that you use or hear often?

Practice 4: Identifying Hyperboles

A. Choose the statement that expresses the literal meaning of each hyperbole.

1. When I heard that joke, I nearly died laughing.

    A. The joke was so funny that it killed the listener.

    B. The joke was extremely funny.

    C. The joke was so painful it killed the listener.

    D. The joke made the listener sick.

2. I've seen that movie a million times.

    A. I've seen that movie too many times to count.

    B. I have literally seen that movie 1,000,000 times.

    C. I enjoy that movie every time I see it.

    D. none of these

3. We stood in line for an eternity.

    A. We are still standing in line.

    B. We never stood in line.

    C. We were in line for a very long time.

    D. We died while standing in line.

4. Dirty dishes were piled up to the ceiling.

   A. Dishes were literally stacked so high that they reached the ceiling.

   B. There was an overwhelming pile of dirty dishes.

   C. The low ceiling in the room meant that the dishes reached to the ceiling.

   D. none of these

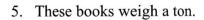

5. These books weigh a ton.

   A. There are a ton of books.

   B. The books literally weigh a ton.

   C. The books are very heavy.

   D. none of these

B. With a classmate, discuss the meaning of each of the following hyperboles.

6. I nearly died laughing.

7. She was hopping mad.

8. I was so hungry, I could eat a horse.

9. He's as big as a house.

10. When he saw the bear, his jaw dropped to his knees.

PERSONIFICATION

Using **personification**, an author gives human qualities to an animal, object, or idea. The comic strip "Garfield" has an example of personification. The animal character, Garfield the cat, talks and acts like a human. He even eats lasagna! Can you think of other examples of personification?

Practice 5: Identifying Personification

Read the following passages from *The Wind in the Willows* by Kenneth Grahame, paying attention to the writer's use of personification.

 The Mole had been working very hard all the morning, spring-cleaning his little home. First with brooms, then with dusters; then on ladders and steps and chairs, with a brush and a pail of whitewash; till he had dust in his throat and eyes, and splashes of whitewash all over his black fur, and an aching back and weary arms.

1. What example of personification is used in this passage?

   A. A house is given human qualities.

   B. A mole is given human qualities.

   C. Chairs and ladders are given human qualities.

   D. A human acts like a mole.

Spring was moving in the air above and in the earth below and around him, penetrating even his dark and lowly little house with its spirit of divine discontent and longing.

2. What example of personification is used in this passage?

   A. Spring is given human qualities.

   B. Darkness is given human qualities.

   C. The house is given animal qualities.

   D. This line does not contain personification.

The sunshine struck hot on his fur, soft breezes caressed his heated brow…

3. What example of personification is used in this passage?

   A. The sunshine is given human qualities.

   B. The breeze is given human qualities.

   C. The mole's brow is given human qualities.

   D. both A and B

ALLITERATION

Alliteration is a repetition of consonant sounds at the beginning of words. Words in a phrase that uses alliteration all begin with the same consonant sound. They are sometimes tongue twisters when read or spoken quickly. Can you say this alliterative phrase quickly?

Peter **P**iper **p**icked a **p**eck of **p**ickled **p**eppers.

Practice 6: Identifying Alliteration

A. Read the following poetic passages paying attention to the use of alliteration.

> **(1)** "When my lover calls I haste-
> **(2)** Dame Disdain was never wedded!"
> **(3)** Ripple-ripple round her waist,
> **(4)** Clear the current eddied.
>
> –from Rudyard Kipling's "A Ripple Song"

1. Which line from this stanza does **not** contain alliteration?

   A. Line 1   **B.** Line 2   **C.** Line 3   **D.** Line 4

> **(1)** Foolish heart and faithful hand,
> **(2)** Little feet that touched no land.
> **(3)** Far away the ripple sped,
> **(4)** Ripple—ripple—running red!
>
> –from Rudyard Kipling's "A Ripple Song"

2. Which line from this stanza does **not** contain alliteration?

   A. Line 1   **B.** Line 2   **C.** Line 3   **D.** Line 4

> **(1)** Be patient with you?
> **(2)** When the stooping sky
> **(3)** Leans down upon the hills
> **(4)** And tenderly, as one who soothing stills
> **(5)** An anguish, gathers earth to lie
> **(6)** Embraced and girdled. Do the sun-filled men
> **(7)** Feel patience then?
>
> –from Amy Lowell's "Patience"

3. Which line contains alliteration?

   A. Line 1   **B.** Line 2   **C.** Line 3   **D.** Line 7

(1) The moon, like a flower
(2) In heaven's high bower,
(3) With silent delight,
(4) Sits and smiles on the night.

–from William Blake's "Night"

4.   Which line contains alliteration?

   A. Line 1   **B.** Line 2   **C.** Line 3   **D.** none of these

B. For each of the following, make up something to complete a sentence that uses alliteration.

   5.   Lazy Larry _____.
   6.   Pretty Priscilla _____.
   7.   Greedy Gregory _____.
   8.   Tiny Tim _____.
   9.   Happy Harry _____.

ONOMATOPOEIA

Onomatopoeia is the use of words whose sounds suggest their meanings.

   Examples: *buzz*, *whoosh*, and *sizzle*

When we see the sound of animal noises written out, this is also an example of onomatopoeia. The use of onomatopoeia helps a reader to visualize the words of a story or poem.

Practice 7: Identifying Onomatopoeia

A. Can you think of a word that uses onomatopoeia to go along with each of the following items?

1.   the sound a cat makes

2.   the sound of an old-fashioned clock

3.   the sound of a croaking frog

4.   the sound of an automobile horn

5.   the sound of a revving engine

B. Identify the example of onomatopoeia in each sentence.

1. The buzz of the clock awoke Mandy from her nap.

2. The birds fluttered away to the rooftop.

3. The bang of the fireworks startled the small children.

4. Monte's shot hit the net with a clean, crisp swoosh.

5. Sydney heard the distant meow of her sad kitten.

CHAPTER 6 SUMMARY

- An **idiom** is an expression using words that are not meant to be taken literally. It contains words that people commonly know. The words are used in an uncommon way. For example, *raining cats and dogs*, *cat nap*, and *cat's got your tongue*, are all examples of idioms.

- Writers often use **metaphors** for emphasis or explanation. A metaphor is a comparison of two things that are normally not alike. An example of a metaphor would be: *His eyes were huge saucers, spinning in every direction.*

- Like a metaphor, a **simile** is a comparison of two things that are not alike. Unlike a metaphor, a simile always uses the words *like* or *as* to make a comparison. An example of a simile would be: *Mary slept like a baby.*

- **Hyperbole** is exaggeration used for emphasis. Hyperboles are not literally true. They help the writer or speaker emphasize a point. For example, when someone says, "I've told you a thousand times already," this is a hyperbole.

- **Alliteration** is a repetition of consonant sounds at the beginning of words, as in the rhyme, "She sells sea shells by the sea shore."

- **Onomatopoeia** is the use of words whose sounds suggest their meanings. Examples are *buzz*, *whoosh*, and *sizzle*.

CHAPTER 6 REVIEW

1. This sentence (from "The Emperor's New Clothes" by Hans Christian Andersen) contains an example of which of the following?

   Many years ago, there was an Emperor, who was so excessively fond of new clothes, that he spent all his money in dress.

   A. idiom   **B.** metaphor   **C.** simile   **D.** hyperbole

2. This sentence contains an example of which of the following?

   When Molly caught the flu, she was as sick as a dog.

   A. alliteration only   **C.** simile only

   B. hyperbole only   **D.** simile and idiom

3. This sentence contains an example of which of the following?

   Lucy Lin likes looking for lucky lemons.

   A. idiom   **B.** metaphor   **C.** alliteration   **D.** hyperbole

4. The following sentence contains an example of which of the following?

   Every since she was a tot, Abbey had been as stubborn as a mule.

   A. idiom only   **C.** alliteration only

   B. simile and idiom   **D.** idiom and alliteration

5. This sentence contains an example of which of the following?

   The steady whirring of the ceiling fan lulled him to sleep.

   A. idiom   **C.** alliteration

   B. simile   **D.** onomatopoeia

6. The following sentence is an example of which of the following?

   Dino the dinosaur dines on dumplings for dinner.

   A. alliteration   **C.** idiom

   B. onomatopoeia   **D.** hyperbole

7. The following sentence is an example of which of the following?

   This life is a winding road.

   A. alliteration   **B.** metaphor   **C.** simile   **D.** idiom

8. In the following sentence, what is the meaning of the italicized idiom?

> The Yorkie pup has a *bark that is worse than its bite.*

A. The Yorkie pup has a larger bite than most Yorkies of his size tend to have.

B. The Yorkie pup barks all the time.

C. The Yorkie pup's bark makes him seem more vicious than he actually is.

D. none of the above

9. In the following sentence, what is the meaning of the italicized idiom?

> While gathering clues to solve the mystery, the investigator wasted too much time *barking up the wrong tree.*

A. The investigator's dog is barking at a cat in a tree.

B. The investigator is following clues that lead away from the answer to the mystery.

C. The investigator is following clues that will lead directly to the answer to the mystery.

D. none of the above.

10. Read the following passage, an excerpt from "The Princess and the Pea" by Hans Christian Andersen. After reading, identify the *hyperbole* Andersen used.

> There was once a Prince who wished to marry a Princess; but then she must be a real Princess. He traveled all over the world in hopes of finding such a lady; but there was always something wrong. Princesses he found in plenty; but whether they were real Princesses it was impossible for him to decide, for now one thing, now another, seemed to him not quite right about the ladies. At last he returned to his palace quite cast down because he wished so much to have a real Princess for his wife.

A. There was once a Prince who wished to marry a Princess.

B. She must be a real Princess.

C. He traveled all over the world in hopes of finding such a lady.

D. At last he returned to his palace quite cast down.

11. Read the following passage from Hans Christian Andersen's "The Real Princess" After reading, identify the *simile*.

One evening a fearful tempest arose. It thundered and lightened, and the rain poured down from the sky in torrents. Besides, it was as dark as pitch. All at once there was heard a violent knocking at the door, and the old King, the Prince's father, went out himself to open it.

A. One evening a fearful tempest arose.

B. It thundered and lightened.

C. The rain poured down from the sky in torrents.

D. It was as dark as pitch.

12. Which figurative language technique is used in the following sentence?

The neighbor's dog howled and barked all might, keeping us all awake.

A. onomatopoeia

B. metaphor

C. simile

D. none of the above

13. In the sentence, the idiom and metaphor "bull in a china shop" means which of the following?

The burly man was a *bull in a china shop*.

A. The man looked a little bit like a bull.

B. A burly man has no place in a china shop.

C. The burly man is clumsy and uncoordinated.

D. none of the above

14. The following sentence is an example of which of the following?

Gary goes grumpily into the garage.

A. alliteration

B. hyperbole

C. onomatopoeia

D. idiom

15. Read the following poem by Edna St. Vincent Millay. What literary device is used in lines 1 and 3?

Second April

1 **To what purpose, April, do you return again?**
2 Beauty is not enough.
3 **You can no longer quiet me with the redness**
4 Of little leaves opening stickily.
5 I know what I know.
6 The sun is hot on my neck as I observe
7 The spikes of the crocus.
8 The smell of the earth is good.

A. alliteration

B. personification

C. onomatopoeia

D. hyperbole

16. Read the following passage from Rudyard Kipling's "The Beginning of the Armadillos," and decide which element is used for the animal characters in the passage.

 THIS, O Best Beloved, is another story of the High and Far-Off Times. In the very middle of those times was a Stickly-Prickly Hedgehog, and he lived on the banks of the turbid Amazon, eating shelly snails and things. And he had a friend, a Slow-Solid Tortoise, who lived on the banks of the turbid Amazon, eating green lettuces and things. And so that was all right, Best Beloved. Do you see?

But also, and at the same time, in those High and Far-Off Times, there was a Painted Jaguar, and he lived on the banks of the turbid Amazon too; and he ate everything that he could catch. When he could not catch deer or monkeys, he would eat frogs and beetles; and when he could not catch frogs and beetles, he went to his Mother Jaguar, and she told him how to eat hedgehogs and tortoises.

She said to him ever so many times, graciously waving her tail, "My son, when you find a Hedgehog, you must drop him into the water and then he will uncoil, and when you catch a Tortoise, you must scoop him out of his shell with your paw." And so that was all right, Best Beloved.

A. alliteration

B. simile

C. metaphor

D. personification

Chapter 7
Basic Elements of Story Structure

This chapter addresses the following Georgia Performance Standards for reading:

ELA6R1	The student demonstrates comprehension and shows evidence of a warranted and responsible explanation of a variety of literary and informational texts.
	e. Identifies and analyzes the elements of setting, characterization, plot, and the resolution of the conflict of a story or play:
	i. internal/external conflicts
	ii. character conflicts, characters vs. nature, characters vs. society
	iii. antagonist/protagonist.

In most stories, there are some basic elements. These elements are very important because they provide a structure that readers unconsciously understand. Think of the last book that you read. Where did the story take place? Who were the characters? What happened? What problems did the characters encounter? If you can answer these questions, then you already understand some things about the basic elements of story structure. In this chapter, you will learn about common elements of story structure and discover how these elements affect the development of the fiction that we read. Let's begin with a look at the element of setting.

SETTING

Setting is the time and place of action for a literary work. A story may take place in any era—past, present, or future. Also, a story may take place in any part of the world, real or imagined. Smaller aspects of setting might be specific places such as a middle school, the mall, or a baseball field. Setting is very important because when and where the action of a story occurs directly affects other elements in the story. For example, if you read a story with a historical setting, how might the action and ideas of the characters differ from those in a story set in the present day or in the future?

One way to identify setting in fiction that you read is to look for clues to help you know something about the time period or the place of action. Read the following passage, paying attention to any clues that might help you to know about the setting.

> Shauna looked around at the desks in Ms. West's classroom. They were different from the desks at her old middle school in Philadelphia. Instead of the desk part being connected to the chair, with a wire basket underneath, the chair and desk were two separate parts. The desk had a wide opening for books, a notch for a pencil, and a wooden top. The desks weren't the only difference she noticed here. She thought about the groups of sixth graders she had seen milling about in the cafeteria yesterday morning. Some of them stood around in small groups chatting. Others listened to their iPods. No one seemed really angry, though. In a way, things were actually calm and peaceful.

If you had to identify a time period for this story, what clue(s) might help you to do so? One thing that you could identify right away is the mention of iPods. This helps the reader to identify the time setting as the modern day, as iPods have not been around for very long. Can you find any other clues about the time period? Where does this part of the story take place? If you answered that it takes place in a middle school, then you are correct. Based on the details provided, the reader can say that the story is set in a modern-day middle school.

Practice 1: Setting

Read the passages, looking for details about the story's setting. Answer the questions that follow each passage.

> Rose sat all alone in the big best parlor, with her little handkerchief laid ready to catch the first tear, for she was thinking of her troubles, and a shower was expected. She had retired to this room as a good place in which to be miserable; for it was dark and still, full of ancient furniture, sombre curtains, and hung all around with portraits of solemn old gentlemen in wigs, severe-nosed ladies in top-heavy caps, and staring children in little bob-tailed coats or short-waisted frocks. It was an excellent place for woe; and the fitful spring rain that pattered on the window-pane seemed to sob, "Cry away: I'm with you."
>
> –from *Eight Cousins* by Louisa May Alcott

1. Which of the following **best** describes the story's setting?

  A. modern day

  B. in the pre-historic past

  C. future times

  D. in the not too distant historical past

2. Where does the scene of this passage occur?

    A. in the master bedroom   **C.** in the parlor

    B. in the kitchen   **D.** none of these

It was seven o'clock of a very warm evening in the Seeonee hills when Father Wolf woke up from his day's rest, scratched himself, yawned, and spread out his paws one after the other to get rid of the sleepy feeling in their tips. Mother Wolf lay with her big gray nose dropped across her four tumbling, squealing cubs, and the moon shone into the mouth of the cave where they all lived. "Augrh!" said Father Wolf. "It is time to hunt again." He was going to spring down hill when a little shadow with a bushy tail crossed the threshold and whined: "Good luck go with you, O Chief of the Wolves. And good luck and strong white teeth go with noble children that they may never forget the hungry in this world."

–from Rudyard Kipling's *The Jungle Book*

3. The setting of this story is

    A. a zoo.   **C.** a large city.

    B. the wilderness.   **D.** the circus.

4. In this passage, the time of day is

    A. evening.   **B.** morning.   **C.** afternoon.   **D.** 7:00 a.m.

CHARACTERIZATION

Another important aspect of story structure is **characterization**. Characterization is the way writers use details to show the characters in their stories. Characters can be people, animals, or imaginary creatures. Each character in a story has personal traits and behaviors just like real people do. In a story, a reader learns about a character through actions, dialogue (conversation), and description. All these ways of giving the reader clues about a character are called characterization. As readers, we must look for these clues—descriptive words, character actions, and conversations—to help us get to know a character. For example, read the following passage, looking for clues about Polly.

But Polly did feel and look very shy, when she was ushered into a room full of young ladies, as they seemed to her, all very much dressed, all talking together, and all turning to examine the new-comer with a cool stare which seemed to be as much the fashion as eye-glasses. They nodded affably when Fanny introduced her, said something civil, and made room for her at the table round which they sat waiting for Monsieur. Several of the more frolicsome were imitating the Grecian Bend, some were putting their heads together over little notes, nearly all were eating confectionery, and the entire twelve chattered like magpies. Being politely supplied with caramels, Polly sat looking and listening, feeling very young and countrified among these elegant young ladies.

–from *An Old-Fashioned Girl* by Louisa May Alcott

What details jumped out at you about Polly? Perhaps, you might say that she was shy; the writer states this directly. Also, based on other details, you might say that Polly is new in the room, and she is unsure about whether others will accept her. When we try to find clues about characters, it is important to look at what the writer states through direct details. It is also important to pay attention to descriptions of character behaviors and the actions and reactions of characters around them.

Practice 2: Characterization

Read the following passages looking for details about the characters being described.

It was snowing tiny flakes when Joel's eyes popped open, and the small, feathery things whirled against the little paned window, as if they would very much like to come in.

"Dave—Dave!" cried Joel, poking him, "get up—it's snowing!"

David's eyes flew quite wide at that, and he sat up at once. "Oh, Joel," he squealed, as he watched the flakes, "ain't they pretty!"

"Um! I guess so," said Joel, springing into his clothes; "they're nice for snowballs and to slide on, anyway."

David reached over for one blue woolen stocking on the floor by the side of the bed, and sat quite still with it in his hand, regarding the snowy whirl.

–from *The Adventures of Joel Pepper* by Margaret Sidney

1. Which of the following words **best** describes Joel?

   A. excited   **B.** angry   **C.** scared   **D.** hungry

Mimi stared at the brown sack on the table in front of her. There was no mystery. It would be her usual peanut butter sandwich and an apple, as she had every Tuesday. Her mom was pretty consistent that way. Out of the corner of her eye, she caught a glimpse of Jackie's pink lunch bag. Mimi didn't want to stare at Jackie, but she was really interested to see what would be for lunch today. It seemed like Jackie's

mom always managed to surprise her perfect daughter with something that Mimi wanted. Yesterday, Mimi had envied Jackie's yellow moon pie. Last week, it was the rolled sandwich cut into cute little mini rolls. Jackie had eaten it slowly, roll by sliced roll. Mimi thought to herself, if she were Jackie's mom, maybe she would be so thoughtful about her daughter's lunches, too. Jackie was truly the picture of perfection. Her clothes always looked new and fashionable, and Mimi, thought, the girl had the face of a young goddess. Why shouldn't she have lunches that were fit for a goddess, too?

2. In this passage, Mimi is characterized as

   A. happy.   **B.** envious.   **C.** sleepy.   **D.** greedy.

3. Jackie is characterized as

   A. perfect.   **B.** upset.   **C.** hungry.   **D.** tired.

PROTAGONIST AND ANTAGONIST

In a story, there is often one character who stands out at the center of the action. Most of the story revolves around this character. This character is called the **protagonist**. Generally, the protagonist is a character that readers like. On the other hand, the **antagonist** is the character that creates a problem for the protagonist. The antagonist character is generally a character that readers do not like.

For example, in the fairy tale, "Little Red Riding Hood," the girl called Little Red Riding Hood is the protagonist. The story revolves around her going to visit her grandmother. The Big Bad Wolf, on the other hand, is the antagonist. He eats Little Red Riding Hood's grandmother, and then dresses in her clothes and waits for Little Red, planning to eat her too. He is an enemy to Little Red Riding Hood and causes problems for her.

Protagonists can be more than one person. For example, in a story about a town fighting a band of robbers, the entire town could be considered the protagonists. And antagonists can be something other than people. For instance, in *A Christmas Carol* by Charles Dickens, the antagonist could be the greed that Scrooge feels until Christmas ghosts teach him a lesson.

Can you think of other examples of protagonists and antagonists in stories that you have read?

Practice 3: Protagonist and Antagonist

Discuss with a classmate the plot line of each of the following fairy tales. Decide who the protagonist is. Is it more than one person? Who (or what) is the antagonist?

1. Hansel and Gretel

2. Jack and the Beanstalk

3. Snow White

4. Cinderella

CONFLICT

Another important literary element is **conflict**. Conflict is a problem that occurs in a story or novel. Sometimes, it is an external problem between two characters, such as a disagreement or a physical fight. In other cases, characters have problems that are caused by outside forces like nature or society. Then, there are conflicts that occur internally, such as in the minds of characters. Let's take a closer look at some of these conflicts.

The names for these conflict types are the ones used by scholars for many years. Even though each one says, "man vs.," "man" refers to any character (male, female, animal, imaginary).

MAN VS. SELF

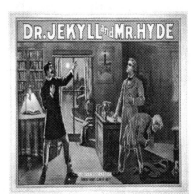

Man vs. self conflicts occur when characters feel undecided or conflicted about something. They are unsure of a decision to make, or feel tormented. This inner questioning is called man vs. self conflict. This type of conflict is internal because it occurs in the mind of a character.

Example: In *Dr. Jekyll and Mr. Hyde* by Robert Louis Stevenson, the main character struggles between two sides of his own personality.

MAN VS. MAN

Man vs. man conflict is external. This occurs outside of a character. In the case of man vs. man conflicts, a character has a problem that involves another character. An example would be two characters who have a physical fight. Even if characters disagree verbally or simply have some sort of conflict with one another, it is still considered to be a man vs. man, external conflict.

>**Example:** In *The Red Badge of Courage* by Stephen Crane, armies of soldiers fight each other.

MAN VS. NATURE

In addition to having problems within self and with others, characters sometimes face problems that are caused by nature. These conflicts, which are also external, may be large natural disaster scenarios such tornadoes, floods, and severe storms that cause problems for a character in a novel or story. Other examples of **man vs. nature** conflicts might be troublesome terrain such as an arid desert that must be crossed or a steep mountain to climb.

>**Example:** In the movie *A Perfect Storm*, the characters try to survive a huge storm out at sea.

MAN VS. SOCIETY

Another external conflict is the **man vs. society** conflict. This type of problem is caused by some social circumstance that affects a character. Examples of man vs. society conflicts include poverty, racism, and classism. When fictional characters are faced with these types of issues, they are in conflict with their society.

>**Example:** In *To Kill a Mockingbird* by Harper Lee, Atticus Finch must defend a client who a racist society already considers guilty.

Practice 4: Conflict

Choose the best answer for each of the following questions.

1. A character who fears public speaking is experiencing which type of conflict?

    A. man vs. self   **C.** man vs. society

    B. man vs. nature   **D.** man vs. man

2. In a historical fiction novel when a family loses a child due to the harsh winter weather, this is an example of which type of conflict?

    A. man vs. self   **C.** man vs. society

    B. man vs. nature   **D.** man vs. man

3. In a story where two characters are members of feuding families, this type of conflict
    would be

    A. man vs. self.   **C.** man vs. society.

    B. man vs. nature.   **D.** man vs. man.

4. In a story where a young mother loses her job because she is unmarried, the
    discrimination problem she faces is an example of which type of conflict?

    A. man vs. self   **C.** man vs. society

    B. man vs. nature   **D.** man vs. man

PLOT

Plot is what actually happens in a story or novel. It is the sequence of events from the beginning
to the end. A story's plot has the following elements: introduction, rising action, climax, falling
action, and resolution. Let's take a look at each of these.

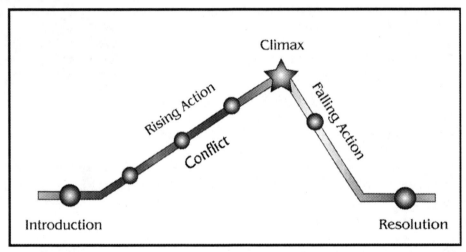

INTRODUCTION

In a story, the **introduction** sets the stage for the action and events to come. This part, which
comes at the beginning, includes the setting and an introduction of the story's characters. Also,
it is here that conflicts, or problems that characters face, are revealed. In a short story, the
introduction usually is in the first paragraph or two. In a novel, it might happen over the first
couple of chapters.

RISING ACTION

As the plot of a story unfolds, problems occur between opposing forces. We see **rising action** as these problems complicate the lives of the story's characters and are part of the rising action. These problems are called conflicts. Conflicts can occur within the mind of a character or between a character and someone or something else. (Review the previous section about conflicts for more details.)

CLIMAX

The highest point of action in a story is called the **climax**. At this point, a reader's suspense is at its greatest. The climax is also the turning point. That means the action reaches a peak and begins to move toward resolution.

FALLING ACTION

After the story's highest point of action, or climax, the story begins to move toward resolution. This is called **falling action**. Solutions seem to arise for major conflicts, and the details of plot begin to wrap up.

RESOLUTION

The **resolution** is the end of a story. The conflict is resolved, and loose ends are tied up.

Practice 5: Plot

Read the passage and answer the questions that follow.

The Lion's Share

The Lion once went hunting along with the Fox, the Jackal, and the Wolf. They hunted and they hunted, until at last they surprised a Stag, and soon they caught it. Then came the question how the spoil should be divided. "Quarter me this Stag," roared the Lion; so the other animals skinned it and cut it into four parts. Then the Lion took his stand in front of the carcass and pronounced judgment. "The first quarter is for me in my capacity as King of Beasts; the second is mine as judge; another share comes to me for my part in the chase; and as for the fourth quarter, well, as for that, I should like to see which of you will dare to lay a paw upon it."

"Humph," grumbled the Fox. as he walked away with his tail between his legs. But he spoke in a low growl "You may share the labors of the great, but you will not share the rewards."

–from Aesop's fables

1. Which of the following **best** summarizes the plot of the fable?

    A. A lion, fox, jackal, and wolf hunt a stag. They all share the rewards of the kill.

    B. A lion, fox, jackal, and wolf hunt a stag. The lion takes the rewards of the kill for himself.

    C. A lion, fox, jackal, and stag share a hunt. The lion takes the rewards for himself.

    D. A lion, fox, jackal, and wolf hunt a stag. They divide the rewards of the kill between them.

2. What part of the plot is the following section?

    > They hunted and they hunted, until at last they surprised a Stag, and soon they caught it. Then came the question how the spoil should be divided.

    A. introduction   **C.** climax

    B. rising action   **D.** falling action

3. Which two of the following is a conflict that occurs in the fable?

    A. The animals argue about who should kill the stag. This is an external conflict.

    B. The animals have an internal conflict about whether or not to kill the stag.

    C. The fox is upset with the lion for not sharing the spoils. This is an external conflict.

    D. The lion tries to decide whether or not to claim all of the spoils. This is an internal conflict.

The Man and the Wood

A Man came into a Wood one day with an axe in his hand, and begged all the Trees to give him a small branch which he wanted for a particular purpose. The Trees were good-natured and gave him one of their branches. What did the Man do but fix it into the axe head and soon set to work cutting down tree after tree. Then the Trees saw how foolish they had been in giving their enemy the means for destroying them.

–from Aesop's fables

4. In this fable, which of the following statements **best** describes the introduction?

   A. A man who lives near the forest dislikes trees, so he is in conflict with them.

   B. A man goes into the woods one day, and he asks the trees for a branch.

   C. A bunch of trees in a forest are given human qualities.

   D. A man uses an axe to chop down a forest.

5. The following section of the story makes up what part of the plot?

   > What did the Man do but fix it into the axe head and soon set to work cutting down tree after tree.

   A. introduction
   C. climax

   B. rising action
   D. resolution

CHAPTER 7 SUMMARY

- **Setting** is the time and place of action for a literary work.

- **Characterization** is how a writer presents characters in a story. Characters are people, animals, or imaginary creatures. A reader learns about characters through actions, dialogue, and description. The process of giving the reader clues about a character is called characterization.

- The **protagonist and antagonist** are two important characters (or groups) in a story. The protagonist is the main character at the center of the storyline. Generally, the protagonist is a character that readers like. The antagonist is the character that creates a problem for the protagonist. The antagonist can also be something in nature, in society, or even in the protagonist's mind.

- **Plot** is what happens in the story. It is the sequence of events from the beginning to the end. A story's plot has the following elements: **introduction, rising action, climax, falling action,** and **resolution.**

CHAPTER 7 REVIEW

Read the passage, and answer the questions that follow.

The Tale of Peter Rabbit

Once upon a time there were four little Rabbits, and their names were—Flopsy, Mopsy, Cotton-tail, and Peter. They lived with their Mother in a sandbank, underneath the root of a very big fir-tree.

"Now, my dears," said old Mrs. Rabbit one morning, "you may go into the fields or down the lane, but don't go into Mr. McGregor's garden: your Father had an accident there; he was put in a pie by Mrs. McGregor."

"Now run along, and don't get into mischief. I am going out."

Then old Mrs. Rabbit took a basket and her umbrella, and went through the wood to the baker's. She bought a loaf of brown bread and five currant buns.

Flopsy, Mopsy, and Cotton-tail, who were good little bunnies, went down the lane to gather blackberries; But Peter, who was very naughty, ran straight away to Mr. McGregor's garden, and squeezed under the gate!

First he ate some lettuces and some French beans; and then he ate some radishes; And then, feeling rather sick, he went to look for some parsley.

But round the end of a cucumber frame, whom should he meet but Mr. McGregor! Mr. McGregor was on his hands and knees planting out young cabbages, but he jumped up and ran after Peter, waving a rake and calling out, "Stop thief."

Peter was most dreadfully frightened; he rushed all over the garden, for he had forgotten the way back to the gate. He lost one of his shoes among the cabbages, and the other shoe amongst the potatoes.

After losing them, he ran on four legs and went faster, so that I think he might have got away altogether if he had not unfortunately run into a gooseberry net, and got caught by the large buttons on his jacket. It was a blue jacket with brass buttons, quite new.

Peter gave himself up for lost and shed big tears; but his sobs were overheard by some friendly sparrows, who flew to him in great excitement, and implored him to exert himself.

Mr. McGregor came up with a sieve, which he intended to pop upon the top of Peter; but Peter wriggled out just in time, leaving his jacket behind him. And rushed into the tool shed, and jumped into a can. It would have been a beautiful thing to hide in, if it had not had so much water in it.

Mr. McGregor was quite sure that Peter was somewhere in the tool shed, perhaps hidden underneath a flower-pot. He began to turn them over carefully, looking under each.

Presently Peter sneezed—"Kerty-schoo!" Mr. McGregor was after him in no time, And tried to put his foot upon Peter, who jumped out of a window, upsetting three plants. The window was too small for Mr. McGregor, and he was tired of running after Peter. He went back to his work.

Peter sat down to rest; he was out of breath and trembling with fright, and he had not the least idea which way to go. Also he was very damp with sitting in that can.

After a time he began to wander about, going lippity-lippity—not very fast, and looking all around. He found a door in a wall; but it was locked, and there was no room for a fat little rabbit to squeeze underneath.

An old mouse was running in and out over the stone doorstep, carrying peas and beans to her family in the wood. Peter asked her way to the gate, but she had such a large pea in her mouth that she could not answer. She only shook her head at him. Peter began to cry.

Then he tried to find his way straight across the garden, but he became more and more puzzled. Presently, he came to a pond where Mr. McGregor filled his water-cans. A white cat was staring at some goldfish; she sat very, very still, but now and then the tip of her tail twitched as if it were alive. Peter thought it best to go away without speaking to her; he had heard about cats from his cousin, little Benjamin Bunny.

He went back towards the tool shed, but suddenly, quite close to him, he heard the noise of a hoe—scr-r-ritch, scratch, scratch, scritch. Peter scuttered underneath the bushes. But presently, as nothing happened, he came out, and climbed upon a wheelbarrow, and peeped over. The first thing he saw was Mr. McGregor hoeing onions. His back was turned towards Peter, and beyond him was the gate!

Peter got down very quietly off the wheelbarrow, and started running as fast as he could go, along a straight walk behind some black-currant bushes. Mr. McGregor caught sight of him at the corner, but Peter did not care. He slipped underneath the gate, and was safe at last in the wood outside the garden.

Mr. McGregor hung up the little jacket and the shoes for a scare-crow to frighten the blackbirds. Peter never stopped running or looked behind him till he got home to the big fir-tree.

He was so tired that he flopped down upon the nice soft sand on the floor of the rabbit-hole, and shut his eyes. His mother was busy cooking; she wondered what he had done with his clothes. It was the second little jacket and pair of shoes that Peter had lost in a fortnight!

I am sorry to say that Peter was not very well during the evening. His mother put him to bed, and made some chamomile tea; and she gave a dose of it to Peter!

"One table-spoonful to be taken at bed-time." But Flopsy, Mopsy, and Cotton-tail had bread and milk and black-berries for supper.

–from *The Tale of Peter Rabbit* by Beatrix Potter

1. Which of the following **best** summarizes the plot of the story?

   A. Four rabbits go on an adventure and find that Peter is the most adventurous of them all.

   B. Peter Rabbit ventures into Mr. McGregor's yard even though his mother tells him not to do so. He has a wild adventure but returns safely.

   C. Flopsy, Mopsy, Peter, and Cotton-tail venture into Mr. McGregor's yard. They venture out for food, and they return safely.

   D. Peter's mother teaches him how to find food safely in Mr. McGregor's yard.

2. Which of the following **best** describes the story's setting?

   A. a large city   C. a space colony

   B. a rural area   D. a construction site

3. The protagonist of this story is

   A. Flopsy.   B. Mopsy.   C. Cotton-tail.   D. Peter.

4. The antagonist in this story is

   A. Mr. McGregor.   C. Flopsy.

   B. Peter.   D. Peter's mother.

5. Which of the following is a characteristic of Peter Rabbit?

   A. He is shy.   C. He is forgetful.

   B. He is lonely.   D. He is naughty.

6. Which of the following is a characteristic of Peter's mother?

   A. She is hungry.   C. She is wise.

   B. She is forgetful.   D. She is silly.

7. Which of the following **best** characterizes Mr. McGregor?

   A. He is a construction worker at a building site.

   B. He tends his garden.

   C. He is someone who owns a fir tree.

   D. He is a zoo keeper.

8. Which of the following is a conflict that occurs in the story?

    A. Man vs. self: Peter struggles to be a good rabbit.

    B. Man vs. man: Peter has to get away from Mr. McGregor.

    C. Man vs. nature: Peter gets lost and ends up in Mr. McGregor's garden.

    D. Man vs. society: None of the other rabbits understand how hungry Peter is.

9. Which of the following is **not** a part of the story's introduction?

    A. A mother rabbit lives in a sand-bank under a fir-tree with four rabbit children.

    B. Mr. McGregor once put Peters' father in a pie.

    C. Peter is the fastest runner in his rabbit family.

    D. None of these

10. Which of the following is **most likely** the story's climax?

    A. when old Mrs. Rabbit explains what happened to Peter's father

    B. when Peter reaches the rabbit hole

    C. when Peter comes face-to-face with Mr. McGregor

    D. when Peter has to have tea for supper

11. How is the story's action resolved?

    A. Peter suffers the same fate as his father.

    B. Peter makes it home safely.

    C. Mr. McGregor is still looking for Peter.

    D. Peter's mother looks for him and is caught by Mr. McGregor.

12. What is Peter's punishment for running away?

    A. He has to go back and get his coat and shoes off of the scarecrow.

    B. He gets sick and can have nothing but chamomile tea for supper.

    C. He watches Flopsy, Mopsy, and Cotton-tail have dessert while he has none.

    D. He gets a spanking from Mrs. Rabbit and is grounded for a week.

Chapter 8
Advanced Elements of Story Structure

This chapter addresses the following Georgia Performance Standards for reading:

ELA6R1	The student demonstrates comprehension and shows evidence of a warranted and responsible explanation of a variety of literary and informational texts.
	For literary texts, the student identifies the characteristics of various genres and produces evidence of reading that:
	b. Identifies and analyzes the author's use of dialogue and description.
	c. Relates a literary work to historical events of the period.
	d. Applies knowledge of the concept that theme refers to the message about life and the world that the author wants us to understand whether implied or stated
	f. Identifies the speaker and recognizes the difference between first- and third-person narration.
ELA6RC2	The student participates in discussions related to curricular learning in all subject areas. The student:
	a. Identifies messages and themes from books in all subject areas.

In the last chapter, you learned about some basic elements of story structure. In this chapter, you will expand what you learned about how writers create stories by looking at some more advanced story elements. These include dialogue, description, historical setting, point of view, and underlying meaning (theme and message). Let's begin with a look at dialogue.

DIALOGUE

How do we learn about the people, places, and action in a story? Can we look at pictures and know what characters think? How do we know what someone looks like and what the setting is like?

As readers, we must depend upon what characters say and descriptions given by the author to understand a story. What characters say is called **dialogue**. It is just like conversation in real life. Dialogue is a conversation between people. Look at the following example of dialogue taken from Kenneth Grahame's *The Wind in the Willows*.

"The hour has come!" said the Badger at last with great solemnity.

"What hour?" asked the Rat uneasily, glancing at the clock on the mantelpiece.

"*Whose* hour, you should rather say," replied the Badger. "Why, Toad's hour! The hour of Toad! I said I would take him in hand as soon as the winter was well over, and I'm going to take him in hand today!"

"Toad's hour, of course!" cried the Mole delightedly. "Hooray! I remember now! *We'll* teach him to be a sensible Toad!"

This dialogue is between Badger, Rat, and Mole. They are discussing Toad. The details of their conversation show that something important will happen to Toad. In addition, we can infer that Badger is a "take charge" sort of character, while Rat and Mole are followers. In reading dialogue, it is important to pay attention to both what the characters say about events and other characters and to finding clues about the characters who are doing the talking. We do this by reading carefully and paying attention to details provided by the writer.

Practice 1: Dialogue

Read the following passage, paying attention to the writer's use of dialogue. Answer the questions that follow.

The D-halls were clear, and most students were just starting their 4th period classes. Best friends Amber and Melanie sat across from each other in Mrs. Bickell's 4th period language arts class doing their journaling activity for the period. At least, they were supposed to be writing in their journals. Actually, the furious writing of their matching furry pink pens meant that they were writing notes to each other. After about a minute of note writing, there was a knock at the classroom door. Mrs. Bickell stepped quietly outside the door. This was an opportunity to chat!

"So, what happened in math today? Did Mr. Williams collect our homework," Amber whispered to Melanie.

"He checked it in our seats. Then we did word problems with partners," Melanie answered, looking away quickly, hoping her chatty friend would stop talking so that she could really do her own work.

"Well, I didn't do mine. Can I copy yours?"

Melanie thought for a few seconds, searching for a way to say no to Amber without hurting their friendship.

"Well?" Amber questioned impatiently, rushing her. "Hurry up before Ms. Bickell gets back."

"I really didn't finish mine, and it's not right," Melanie added with a nervous giggle.

"Something is better than nothing. Let me see what you have." Amber was relentless.

"No, I don't think so," Melanie said, her voice unsure, almost like a question.

"Come on! Remember, I saved you a seat on the bus yesterday," Amber reminded her friend with a pleading look and raised eyebrows. Just then, Ms. Bickell returned, ready to start class. The girls went back to writing vigorously.

1. Why are the girls whispering?

   A. They are trading secrets.

   B. They are supposed to be working quietly.

   C. They are spreading rumors about a nearby classmate.

   D. none of these

2. Which of the girls appears to be pushy?

   A. Melanie   B. Amber   C. neither one

3. Which of the girls is uncomfortable with the conversation?

   A. Melanie   B. Amber   C. neither one

4. Which statement **best** summarizes the dialogue between Melanie and Amber?

   A. The girls discuss the pros and cons of Mr. Williams' math class.

   B. The girls make plans to complete math homework together.

   C. Amber pressures Melanie to share her math homework, but Melanie is reluctant.

   D. none of these

5. Which part of the conversation most shows that Melanie wants to keep Amber as a friend, even though she knows that copying homework is wrong?

   A. Melanie pauses to think when Amber asks for her math homework.

   B. Melanie giggles nervously at Amber.

   C. Melanie remembers how Amber saved her a seat on the bus yesterday.

   D. Melanie tells Amber that her homework is only partly finished.

DESCRIPTION

In addition to dialogue, writers use **description** to give readers important details. The description may be about a character, setting, plot, or another significant part of the story. These descriptions help readers to picture, relate to, and understand the story. Descriptions give details of what people or places look like, what expressions characters wear as they speak, and what actions are taking place. Without description, our reading would be very boring. It would also be difficult to picture what is going on.

Practice 2: Description

Read the following passage from Lewis Carroll's *Alice's Adventures in Wonderland*, paying attention to the description used. Answer the questions that follow.

The rabbit-hole went straight on like a tunnel for some way, and then dipped suddenly down, so suddenly that Alice had not a moment to think about stopping herself before she found herself falling down a very deep well.

Either the well was very deep, or she fell very slowly, for she had plenty of time as she went down to look about her and to wonder what was going to happen next. First, she tried to look down and make out what she was coming to, but it was too dark to see anything; then she looked at the sides of the well, and noticed that they were filled with cupboards and book-shelves; here and there she saw maps and pictures hung upon pegs. She took down a jar from one of the shelves as she passed; it was labeled '*Orange Marmalade*', but to her great disappointment it was empty: she did not like to drop the jar for fear of killing somebody, so managed to put it into one of the cupboards as she fell past it.

1. Which of the following **best** describes the shape of the rabbit-hole?

    A. wide and winding most of the way

    B. straight and tunnel-like before dipping

    C. circular and narrow all the way

    D. zigzagged most of the way

2. Which of the following **best** describes Alice's fall down the well?

    A. It was fast and scary.

    B. It was slow and gave her time to look around.

    C. It was fast at times, but slow at other times.

    D. none of these

HISTORICAL SETTING

You will remember from chapter 7 that the setting of the story is where the story takes place. Simply put, it is the time and the place of the action. Setting is important because it shapes both character and plot in a story. Sometimes, the setting of a fiction or non-fiction story takes place in the past during an important time in history. This is called **historical setting**. The fact that the story takes place in the past is significant because historical events and periods shape the people who live through them. For example, imagine that 500 years have passed, and people look back on the era in which you lived. What do you think they would say about the way in which your era shaped you?

Historical setting is important in both fiction and nonfiction. For example, *The Diary of Anne Frank*, which is a nonfiction novel, contains the writing of a young girl who lived during the time of the Holocaust. The time and place in which she lived shaped her life and experiences. On the other hand, *The Witch of Blackbird Pond*, which is a fiction novel, is set in 1687. This is the story of a young girl named Kit who goes to live in Connecticut. The historical setting of this book is important in terms of religious beliefs, day-to-day events, and the roles of women and children. Kit's experiences in the book reflect the details of the novel's historical setting.

Practice 3: Historical Setting

Read the following passage from Mark Twain's *The Adventures of Tom Sawyer*, paying attention to clues that inform you about the story's historical setting.

Tom appeared on the sidewalk with a bucket of whitewash and a long-handled brush. He surveyed the fence, and all gladness left him and a deep melancholy settled down upon his spirit. Thirty yards of board fence nine feet high. Life to him seemed hollow, and existence but a burden. Sighing, he dipped his brush and passed it along the topmost plank; repeated the operation; did it again; compared the insignificant whitewashed streak with the far-reaching continent of unwhitewashed fence, and sat down on a tree-box discouraged. Jim came skipping out at the gate with a tin pail, and singing *Buffalo Gals*. Bringing water from the town pump had always been hateful work in Tom's eyes, before, but now it did not strike him so. He remembered that there was company at the pump.

1. Which detail from the excerpt places the setting in the early to mid 1800s?

    A. Tom is on a sidewalk, which people do not use anymore.

    B. The name Jim is not common in more modern times.

    C. The name Tom is not common in more modern times.

    D. There is a mention of a town water pump.

2. Which additional detail from the novel excerpt places the setting in the early to mid 1800s?

    A. There is a mention of a large fence.

    B. Jim sings a song called "Buffalo Gals."

    C. Tom is given the task of painting a fence.

    D. Tom seems depressed.

> The young personage whose proper name had been corrupted into Toady, was a small boy of ten or eleven, apple-cheeked, round-eyed, and curly-headed; arrayed in well-worn, gray knickerbockers, profusely adorned with paint, glue, and shreds of cotton.
>
> –from Louisa May Alcott's "Aunt Kipp"

3. In this sentence, what detail informs the reader of a historical setting?

    A. The character described is named Toady.

    B. The boy is described as being apple-cheeked.

    C. The boy wears "knickerbockers."

    D. none of these

> Little Content, traveling in the care of a lady who had known her aunt and happened to be coming East, had six large trunks, besides a hat-box and two suitcases and a nailed-up wooden box containing odds and ends. Content made quite a sensation when she arrived and her baggage was piled on the station platform.
>
> –from Mary E. Wilkins Freeman's "Big Sister Sally"

4. In this passage, which detail informs the reader of a historical setting?

    A. The girl travels by train.

    B. The girl's name is Content.

    C. The girl carries a hat-box and a wooden box as luggage.

    D. both A and C

SPEAKER AND POINT OF VIEW

Every story has a narrator. The narrator is the **speaker** that tells the story to the reader. Two types of narration are **first person** and the **third person**. The type of narrator used is also referred to as **point of view**.

The first-person narrator tells the story from his/her point of view. A first-person narrator is a character that tells the story as he or she lives through it. This narrator is able to give the reader special insight into the story because he/she participates in the story. As a reader, it is easy to recognize a first-person narrator because this narrator uses the pronoun *I*.

The third-person narrator uses third-person pronouns such as *he, she,* or *they*. The third-person narrator is an unnamed personality who stands back from the story as it is told. Such a narrator may tell the reader exactly what happens with no added insight. On the other hand, some third-person narrators also tell readers what characters want, fear, and think.

Speaker	Type of Narrator	Signal Words	Example
a character	first person	I, we	I love to spend such pleasant Sabbaths, from morning till night, behind the curtain of my open window. (from "Sunday at Home" by Nathaniel Hawthorne)
unknown	third person	he, she, they	As she said this she looked down at her hands, and was surprised to see that she had put on one of the Rabbit's little white kid gloves while she was talking. (from *Alice's Adventures in Wonderland* by Lewis Carroll)

Practice 4: Speaker and Point of View

Read the passages, paying attention to narration. Answer the questions that follow.

Alice was beginning to get very tired of sitting by her sister on the bank, and of having nothing to do: once or twice she had peeped into the book her sister was reading, but it had no pictures or conversations in it, "and what is the use of a book," thought Alice "without pictures or conversation?"

–from *Alice's Adventures in Wonderland* by Lewis Carroll

1. This story uses a _____-person narrator.

   A. first   **B.** second   **C.** third   **D.** fourth

2. Who is the narrator (speaker)?

   A. Alice   **C.** an unknown narrator

   B. her sister   **D.** the book Alice is holding

I loved the old man. He had never wronged me. He had never given me insult. For his gold I had no desire. I think it was his eye! yes, it was this! He had the eye of a vulture—a pale blue eye, with a film over it. Whenever it fell upon me, my blood ran cold; and so by degrees—very gradually—I made up my mind to take the life of the old man, and thus rid myself of the eye forever.

–from "The Tell-Tale Heart" by Edgar Allan Poe

3. This story uses a _____-person narrator.

   A. first   **B.** second   **C.** third   **D.** fourth

4. The narrator in this story is

   A. a character living through the events.

   B. the old man with the strange eye.

   C. an unknown speaker.

   D. no one.

The freshening wind tugged at Fenella's skirts; she went back to her grandma. To her relief grandma seemed no longer sad. She had put the two sausages of luggage one on top of the other, and she was sitting on them, her hands folded, her head a little on one side.

–from "The Voyage" by Katherine Mansfield

5. This story uses a _____-person narrator.

   A. first   **C.** first and third

   B. third   **D.** This story does not use a narrator.

6. Who is the narrator of this story?

   A. Fenella

   B. an unknown speaker

   C. Fenella's grandmother

   D. someone watching Fenella and her grandmother

> Sure you're done with it?"
>
> "Oh, yes," replied the girl, the suggestion of a smile on her face, and in her voice the suggestion of a tear. "Yes; I was just going."
>
> But she did not go. She turned instead to the end of the alcove and sat down before a table placed by the window. Leaning her elbows upon it she looked about her through a blur of tears.
>
> –from "For the Love of the Hills" by Susan Glaspell

7. This story uses a _____-person narrator.

   A. first

   B. third

   C. first and third

   D. This story does not use a narrator.

THEME AND MESSAGE

The terms **theme** and **message** refer to the big ideas that authors seek to express through their writing. Theme is an author's underlying message in a work of literature. The term "theme" is usually applied to fiction literature. The term "message" refers to the underlying big ideas expressed in nonfiction writing. Let's take a look at each.

THEME

Theme refers to the message about life and the world that the author wants us to understand. When reading a work of fiction, you can determine theme by looking for big ideas about life, the world, and human nature. Theme can be **stated directly**—this means that the author tells you what the big idea is, like the lesson in a fable by Aesop. Or, it can be **implied**—this means that the author gives clues but doesn't come right out and tell you the big idea. Look at what happens in the story and what characters learn. That way, you can usually come up with a statement about what the big idea is. Sometimes themes are lessons stories teach. Other times, they are simply observations about life.

Themes in literature are usually not directly stated by the writer. They are usually implied. Rather, it is the job of the reader to seek out and identify a story's theme. To identify a story's theme, a good reader will:

- Pay attention to titles.
- Pay attention to how characters behave, what their traits are, and what they learn.
- Pay attention to key elements of plot (such as conflicts) that point to a big idea.

Here is an example. In a novel called *Tangerine*, writer Edward Bloor tells the story of Paul Fisher and his family. Tangerine is the city in Florida where the Fishers make a new life. The reader learns something interesting about Tangerine: While it is a beautiful place, many dark secrets lurk beneath the surface. The same seems to be true of Paul's brother, Eric. On the surface, he seems to be the storybook adolescent. He has good looks and athletic skill. But beneath the surface, Eric is full of darkness and secrets. By using details of plot and narrative description, Bloor presents the theme that <u>appearances can be deceiving</u>. A reader of the novel *Tangerine* can see this theme carried throughout the book.

MESSAGE

The **message** is the big idea in nonfiction literature. It expresses the author's underlying meaning or opinion. Message in nonfiction may or may not be directly stated. If a clear message is not stated, you can figure it out another way. Pay careful attention to the **tone** or **attitude** in the author's writing. A good reader uses clues from the writer's tone and word choices to help identify the message.

Take a look at the following passage, paying attention to the message being presented.

Citizens of Earth have the duty to treat our home with care and respect. Is it respectful to litter or to waste precious resources? When we waste and pollute our water, do we show care for Earth? What would happen if all citizens of the planet were so careless and inattentive? Actually, there are parts of the earth that have already suffered from the horrible effects of pollution and abuse. In some areas, famine, disease, and drought can be directly linked to the way that people of that region have mistreated the land. By being responsible caretakers of the land and resources, all world citizens can make a difference. We can help ensure a healthy Earth.

Take a moment to talk with a partner about the message the writer presents in the passage. Can you state the message in one sentence? It seems that the writer's message is that <u>caring for and respecting the earth are the responsibilities of citizens worldwide</u>.

Practice 5: Theme and Message

Read the story and use clues from the story to choose the statement that best identifies its theme.

The Frogs Desiring a King

The Frogs were living as happy as could be in a marshy swamp that just suited them; they went splashing about caring for nobody and nobody troubling with them. But some of them thought that this was not right, that they should have a king and a proper constitution, so they determined to send up a petition to Jove to give them what they wanted. "Mighty Jove," they cried, "send unto us a king that will rule over us and keep us in order." Jove laughed at their croaking, and threw down into the swamp a huge Log, which came down to the swamp. The Frogs were frightened out of their lives by the commotion made in their midst, and all rushed to the bank to look at the horrible monster; but after a time, seeing that it did not move, one or two of the boldest of them ventured out towards the Log, and even dared to touch it; still it did not move. Then the greatest hero of the Frogs jumped upon the Log and commenced dancing up and down upon it, thereupon all the Frogs came and did the same; and for some time the Frogs went about their business every day without taking the slightest notice of their new King Log lying in their midst. But this did not suit them, so they sent another petition to Jove, and said to him, "We want a real king; one that will really rule over us." Now this made Jove angry, so he sent among them a big Stork that soon set to work gobbling them all up. Then the Frogs repented when it was too late.

–from Aesop's fables

1. **A.** Don't repent when it is too late. If you do, you run the risk of being destroyed.

   B. It is better to have no ruler than to have a cruel ruler.

   C. Logs, frogs, and storks do not get along.

   D. Frogs are like people; they need rulers.

Read the following nonfiction paragraph and identify the statement that best fits as its message.

Sandra Cisneros is a well-known author who uses her Mexican American roots as a backdrop for her colorful writing. Chicago born in 1954, Cisneros had an interesting childhood. She was her parents' only girl of 8 children. As Cisneros grew up, the family spent years living in lower income housing and moving between Mexico and the United States. Her novels, *The House on Mango Street* and *Caramelo* reflect the trials, triumphs, and personal experiences of her interesting coming of age.

2. **A.** Sandra Cisneros had a hard life and an unhappy childhood.

   B. Sandra Cisneros uses the hardships of her life in her literary work.

   C. Sandra Cisneros' family writes about the family life of Mexican Americans.

   D. None of these

Many adolescents are wasteful when it comes to personal spending money. Some teens earn money through jobs such as baby sitting or doing household chores. Rather than saving the money for responsible and future use, some choose to squander the money earned on "quick fix" pleasures such as sweets or games. Allowance money or other money that adolescents earned might be put to better use if it were saved and its spending planned for. What are some other ways that adolescents might make wise use of their money?

3. Which of the following **best** states the message of this nonfiction passage?

   A. Sweet treats and games are "quick fix" pleasures.

   B. Adolescents do not like to save money.

   C. Adolescents would be wise to save money and plan its spending.

   D. Adolescents have many money-making possibilities.

Jeri looked around her at the empty chairs where her friends used to sit for lunch. Misty would always sit on her right and share her two-pack of cupcakes. Amaya was usually in front of her, bobbing her head to the music that she always had in her head. Toni was usually on her left, cutting her PBJ sandwiches into small, dainty squares. "If only I hadn't been such a jerk," Jeri thought to herself. There was no reason for her to have been so horrible to her good friends. She traded them in for a group of seventh-grade girls who she thought were cooler than her crew. But her old friends had been her buddies since Ms. Lipscomb's kindergarten class. Now, as she sat alone, sipping the last of her juice box, she had no friends at all. What would it take to win her real friends back?

4. Which of the following **best** states the theme of this passage?

    A. It is better to have weird friends than to have no friends at all.

    B. Cooler kids will never be your real friends.

    C. Treat friends with kindness and respect, or you will lose them.

    D. Girls rarely keep their friends for very long.

CHAPTER 8 SUMMARY

- **Dialogue** is what characters say to each other. It is just like conversation in real life.

- **Description** is what writers use to give a reader important details. The description may be about a character, setting, plot, or another significant part of the story.

- **Historical setting** is the description of a time and place in the past. Sometimes, the setting of a fiction or nonfiction story takes place in the past during an important time in history. The fact that the story takes place in the past is significant because historical events and periods shape the people who live through them.

- **Speaker and point of view** refer to who is telling a story. The speaker is the **narrator**. The point of view can be **first person** or **third person**. A first-person narrator is a character within the story who tells the story from his/her point of view, using the pronoun *I*. A third-person narrator is an unnamed speaker and uses third-person pronouns such as *he, she,* or *they*. Some third-person narrators tell the reader exactly what happens with no added insight, while other third-person narrators tell readers what characters want, fear, and think.

- **Theme** is the big idea about life and the world that the author wants us to understand. The term "theme" is usually applied to fiction literature. To identify a story's theme, a good reader will:

  - pay attention to titles.
  - pay attention to the characters' behavior and qualities.
  - pay attention to key elements of plot that point to a big idea.

- **Message** is the big idea in nonfiction literature. It expresses the author's underlying meaning or point of view. Look for the author's tone or attitude and choice of words when figuring out the message.

CHAPTER 8 REVIEW

Read each passage and answer the questions that follow.

> I am going to tell a story, one of those tales of astonishing adventures that happened years and years and years ago. Perhaps you wonder why it is that so many stories are told of "once on a time," and so few of these days in which we live; but that is easily explained.
>
> –from L. Frank Baum's *The Enchanted Island of Yew*

1. What narrative point of view is used in this passage?

   A. first person   C. third person

   B. second person   D. fourth person

The Man, the Boy, and the Donkey

A man and his son were once going with their donkey to market. As they were walking along, leading the donkey, a countryman passed them and said, "You fools, what is a donkey for but to ride upon?"

So the man put the boy on the donkey and they went on their way. But soon they passed a group of men, one of whom said, "See that lazy youngster. He lets his father walk while he rides."

So the man ordered his boy to get off, and he got on himself. But they hadn't gone far when they passed two women, one of whom said to the other, "Shame on that lazy lout to let his poor little son trudge along."

Well, the man didn't know what to do, but at last he picked up his boy and also set him on the Donkey. By this time, they had come to the town, and the passers-by began to jeer and point at them. The man stopped and asked what they were scoffing at. The men said: "Aren't you ashamed of yourself for overloading that poor donkey of yours and your hulking son?"

The man and boy got off and tried to think what to do. They thought and they thought, until at last they cut down a pole, tied the donkey's feet to it, and raised the pole and the donkey to their shoulders. They went along amid the laughter of all who met them until they came to Market Bridge. There, the donkey got one of his feet loose, kicked out, and caused the boy to drop his end of the pole. In the struggle, the donkey fell off the bridge, and with his fore-feet tied together, he was drowned.

–from Aesop's fables

2. What narrative point of view is used in this passage?

   A. first person   **C.** third person

   B. second person   **D.** fourth person

3. What is the theme of this passage?

   A. Traveling can lead to danger and death.

   B. By trying to please everyone, you will please no one.

   C. People should never try to carry donkeys.

   D. It is cruel and uncaring to use animals as beasts of burden.

4. Look back at the dialogue in the passage. Which character first suggests that the man should do something different with the donkey?

   A. a countryman   **C.** the man's son

   B. the donkey   **D.** none of these

5. What description do the women use to shame the man into having his son ride the donkey with him?

   A. The women describe the man as being wasteful.

   B. The women describe the man as being evil.

   C. The women describe the man as being lazy.

   D. none of these

      The author of classic novels such as *Little Women* and *Little Men,* Louisa May Alcott was born in 1832 to Amos Bronson and Abigail May Alcott. She was born in a place called Germantown that is now a part of Philadelphia, Pennsylvania. Growing up with three sisters, of whom she was the second youngest, Louisa had a great deal of life experiences to serve as the basis for her work. In fact, the novel for which she is most widely known, *Little Women*, is about the life of four very different sisters—Meg, Jo, Beth, and Amy.

6. What narrative point of view is used in this passage?

   A. first person   **C.** third person

   B. second person   **D.** fourth person

7. What is the message of this passage?

   A. Louisa May Alcott wrote to contribute to her family income.

   B. Louisa May Alcott was an American author of children's books.

   C. Louisa May Alcott used her life experiences as the basis for writing *Little Women*.

   D. Louisa May Alcott received almost all her early education from her father.

8. Based upon the details of the passage, which of the following **best** describes Louisa May Alcott?

   A. A She was a little woman.

   B. B She was a writer of children's literature.

   C. C She based her writing upon her life experiences.

   D. both B and C

I was born a slave on a plantation in Franklin County, Virginia. I am not quite sure of the exact place or exact date of my birth, but at any rate I suspect I must have been born somewhere and at some time. As nearly as I have been able to learn, I was born near a cross-roads post-office called Hale's Ford, and the year was 1858 or 1859. I do not know the month or the day. The earliest impressions I can now recall are of the plantation and the slave quarters—the latter being the part of the plantation where the slaves had their cabins.

My life had its beginning in the midst of the most miserable, desolate, and discouraging surroundings. This was so, however, not because my owners were especially cruel, for they were not, as compared with many others. I was born in a typical log cabin, about fourteen by sixteen feet square. In this cabin I lived with my mother and a brother and sister till after the Civil War, when we were all declared free.

Of my ancestry I know almost nothing. In the slave quarters, and even later, I heard whispered conversations among the colored people of the tortures which the slaves, including, no doubt, my ancestors on my mother's side, suffered in the middle passage of the slave ship while being conveyed from Africa to America. I have been unsuccessful in securing any information that would throw any accurate light upon the history of my family beyond my mother. She, I remember, had a half-brother and a half-sister. In the days of slavery not very much attention was given to family history and family records—that is, black family records. My mother, I suppose, attracted the attention of a purchaser who was afterward my owner and hers. Her addition to the slave family attracted about as much attention as the purchase of a new horse or cow. Of my father I know even less than of my mother. I do not even know his name. I have heard reports to the effect that he was a white man who lived on one of the near-by plantations. Whoever he was, I never heard of his taking the least interest in me or providing in any way for my rearing. But I do not find especial fault with him. He was simply another unfortunate victim of the institution which the Nation unhappily had engrafted upon it at that time.

–from Booker T. Washington's *Up From Slavery*

9. Which of the following **best** states the writer's message?

    A. His was a hard life, filled with trial and hardship.

    B. He enjoyed his childhood.

    C. He had all that he wanted and needed.

    D. He lived the life of a free man, although he was a slave.

10. What point of view does this narrator use?

    A. first person   **C.** third person

    B. second person   **D.** fourth person

11. Which of the following **best** describes the setting of this passage?

    A. the United States during the time of slavery

    B. modern-day United States

    C. the United States during The Great Depression

    D. none of these

12. Based upon the description in the passage, which of the following is **not** true?

    A. The narrator was born a slave.

    B. The narrator was born a free man.

    C. The narrator was born on a plantation.

    D. In the time of slavery, little attention was given to family history.

Chapter 9
Reading and Understanding Literature and Poetry

This chapter addresses the following Georgia Performance Standards for reading:

ELA6R1	The student demonstrates comprehension and shows evidence of a warranted and responsible explanation of a variety of literary and informational texts.
	For literary texts, the student identifies the characteristics of various genres and produces evidence of reading that:
	g. Defines and explains how tone is conveyed in literature through word choice, sentence structure, punctuation, rhythm, repetition, and rhyme.
	h. Responds to and explains the effects of sound, figurative language, and graphics in order to uncover meaning in literature:
	i. Sound (e.g., alliteration, onomatopoeia, rhyme scheme)
	iii. Graphics (i.e., capital letters, line length, bold face print, italics).

What is poetry? Some people think of poetry as rhyming, rhythmic, and filled with imagery. Others see many song lyrics as poetic. Still others realize that the plays of Shakespeare and books like Beowulf also are poetry. They are all correct, yet these examples don't exactly define poetry. Whatever your response about what makes poetry, one thing is for sure: Poetry is emotion-filled literary language. In its many forms, poetry expresses and entertains. Unlike prose, poetry does not have to follow many of the rules of Standard American English.

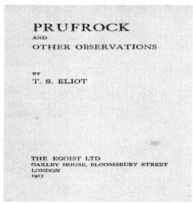

PRUFROCK
AND
OTHER OBSERVATIONS

BY
T. S. ELIOT

THE EGOIST LTD
OAKLEY HOUSE, BLOOMSBURY STREET
LONDON
1917

In this chapter, we will take a look at some elements that writers use to create both literary prose and poetry, and we will discuss qualities specific to poetry. We will begin with a look at tone.

TONE

One element that is an important part of both poetry and prose is **tone**. Tone is the attitude that a writer takes toward the audience, a subject, or a character. Writers convey tone through word choice, sentence structure, punctuation, rhythm, repetition, and rhyme.

For example, a writer's use of exciting words may convey a tone of exhilaration. Short, choppy sentences in a text might be used to convey a writer's attitude of impatience. Let's take a look at some examples.

Dear Mom,

I am having a great time at summer camp! On Mondays, we have been doing crafts, and on Tuesdays and Thursdays, we have gone hiking. One day, we actually saw a family of deer as we trekked through a nearby clearing! Although I am really enjoying myself, I miss home and all of you. I really miss your famous walnut fudge brownies! I can't wait to see you next week during Parent Weekend. I'll see you soon!

Love,

Cal

As you read the letter, you should have noticed that the writer used a tone of happiness and excitement. The word choices were upbeat, and the punctuation (exclamation points) also indicated fun and optimism. Can you go back and pick out specific words that show the writer's happiness and excitement? Here is another example of a writer's use of tone:

All is old
There's nothing new

All is dark
Grey clouded, blue

Feeling sad,
A wasted day,

Waiting for the sun
To chase rain clouds away.

The speaker's tone in the poem is one of sadness and disappointment. Can you identify specific lines, words, or stanzas that express sadness or disappointment?

Practice 1:   Tone

Read each passage, paying attention to the tone of the writer or the speaker. Answer the questions that follow each passage.

> We're strange folks here.
>
> We're tryin' to be cheerful,
>
> An' keep this home from gettin' tearful.
>
> –from Edgar A. Guest's "Just Folks"

1. Which of the following **best** describes the speaker's tone in this stanza?

   A. annoyed   **B.** patient   **C.** surprised   **D.** crabby

> Sweet dreams, form a shade
> O'er my lovely infant's head!
> Sweet dreams of pleasant streams
> By happy, silent, moony beams!
>
> Sweet Sleep, with soft down
> Weave thy brows an infant crown!
> Sweet Sleep, angel mild,
> Hover o'er my happy child!
>
> –from William Blake's "Cradle Song"

2. Which of the following **best** describes the speaker's tone in this poem?

   A. inviting   **B.** sacrificing   **C.** depressed   **D.** irritated

SOUND

Poetry is best when read aloud. This is the case because one characteristic of poetry is the use of **sound devices** to create rhythmic or distinctive patterns in sound. These patterns are most distinct when read aloud. Let's take a look at some common poetic devices that employ sound.

ALLITERATION

One sound device that poets use is called **alliteration**. Alliteration, as you learned in chapter 6, is the repetition of consonant sounds at the beginning of words. For example, in the following poem by William Blake, alliteration is used in lines 1 and 2. There is a repetition of the consonant *l* in the words *little* and *lamb*.

Little lamb, I'll tell thee;
Little lamb, I'll tell thee:
He is called by thy name,
For He calls Himself a Lamb.
He is meek, and He is mild,
He became a little child.
I a child, and thou a lamb,
We are called by His name.
Little lamb, God bless thee!
Little lamb, God bless thee!

Practice 2: Alliteration

Tiger, tiger, burning bright
In the forests of the night,
What immortal hand or eye
Could frame thy fearful symmetry?

1. What lines in this portion of Blake's "Tiger" contains alliteration?

   A. lines 1 and 4   **C.** line 3

   B. line 2   **D.** lines 2 and 3

'TIS little I could care for pearls
   Who own the ample sea;
Or brooches, when the Emperor
   With rubies pelteth me;

Or gold, who am the Prince of Mines;
   Or diamonds, when I see
A diadem to fit a dome
   Continual crowning me.

–"Real Riches" by Emily Dickinson

2. Which of the following phrases from the poem is an example of alliteration?

   A. care for pearls   **C.** continual crowning me

   B. diadem to fit a dome   **D.** both B and C

ONOMATOPOEIA

Another sound device that both writers of prose and poetry use is called **onomatopoeia**. Onomatopoeia, as you also learned in chapter 6, is the use of words whose sounds suggest their meanings. They are sometimes called words that actually make the same sound that they describe. Examples are *boom, swish*, and *tick*. Animal sounds, like *woof* and *meow*, are also examples of onomatopoeia. The use of onomatopoeia helps a reader to form images. Can you identify an example of onomatopoeia from this nursery rhyme?

Baa baa black sheep, have you any wool?
Yes sir, yes sir, three bags full!
One for the master, one for the dame,
And one for the little boy who lives down
the lane.

–Nursery Rhyme

You should have identified the words/sounds "baa, baa" as the sound that a sheep makes.

Practice 3: Onomatopoeia

1 We climb out of bed with a frouzly head

2 And a snarly-yarly voice.

3 We shiver and scowl and we grunt and we growl

4 At our bath and our boots and our toys;

–from Rudyard Kipling's "How the Camel Got His Hump"

1. Which line in the poem contains an example of onomatopoeia?
    A. line 1   **B.** line 2   **C.** line 3   **D.** line 4

"Whew!" said the Djinn, whistling, "that's my Camel, for all the gold in Arabia! What does he say about it?"

"He says 'Humph!'" said the Dog; "and he won't fetch and carry."

"Does he say anything else?"

"Only 'Humph!'; and he won't plough," said the Ox.

2. In this passage from Rudyard Kipling's "How the Camel Got His Hump," which word is an example of onomatopoeia?
    A. plough   **B.** humph   **C.** fetch   **D.** carry

RHYME SCHEME

Rhyme is the repetition of sounds at the end of words. There are many variations of rhyme schemes. Rhymes that occur at the end of a line are called *end rhymes*. Rhymes within a line are called *internal rhymes*. For example, read this poem by William Blake.

1 When voices of children are heard on the green,
2 And laughing is heard on the hill,
3 My heart is at rest within my breast,
4 And everything else is still.
5 "Then come home, my children, the sun is gone down,
6 And the dews of night arise;
7 Come, come, leave off play, and let us away,
8 Till the morning appears in the skies."
9 "No, no, let us play, for it is yet day,
10 And we cannot go to sleep;
11 Besides, in the sky the little birds fly,
12 And the hills are all covered with sheep."
13 "Well, well, go and play till the light fades away,
14 And then go home to bed."
15 The little ones leaped, and shouted, and laughed,
16 And all the hills echoed.

Examples of end rhyme are *hill* and *still* (lines 2 and 4) and *arise* and *skies* (lines 6 and 8). You can find an internal rhyme in line 9, *play* and *day*. You can also find an internal rhyme in line 11, *sky* and *fly*.

To help identify **rhyme scheme** patterns in a poem, we can use letters of the alphabet. To do so, look at a poem and assign a different letter to each different rhyme sound that occurs. When matching sounds occur, repeat a letter. Look at the following example:

Roses are red

Violets are blue

Roses are pretty

And so are you

Line one ends with *red*, so it is assigned the letter **a**.

Line two ends with *blue*. *Blue* does not rhyme with *red*; it is a new rhyme sound, so this line is assigned the letter **b**.

Line three ends with *pretty*. *Pretty* does not rhyme with either *red* or *blue*, so this line is assigned the letter **c**.

Line four ends with *you*. *You* rhymes with *blue*, so this line will also receive a letter **b**.

So, the rhyme scheme of this poem is **abcb**. Take a look at the poem again with the rhyme scheme labeled.

Roses are red   a

Violets are blue   b

Roses are pretty   c

And so are you   b

Practice 4: Rhyme Scheme

Read the poems and identify the rhyme scheme used.

Little lamb, who made thee?
Does thou know who made thee,
Gave thee life, and bid thee feed
By the stream and o'er the mead;

–from "The Lamb" by William Blake

1. What is the rhyme scheme of this portion of the poem?

    A. aabc   **B.** abba   **C.** aabb   **D.** abcd

I lost a world the other day.
Has anybody found?
You'll know it by the row of stars
Around its forehead bound.

2. What type of rhyming is used in this portion of Emily Dickinson's poem?

    A. internal rhyme   **C.** no rhyme

    B. end rhyme   **D.** both A and B

GRAPHICS

Sometimes, in addition to using sound, poets use **graphics**. In poetry, the word *graphics* does not refer to pictures but rather to details that a reader can see which add special emphasis. Graphics are useful because most poems don't come with instructions for reading, like when to say something more loudly or when to stop abruptly. If a poet adds graphic details, this helps you to read the poem as it was written. It also helps you to interpret the meaning of the poem.

Some commonly used poetic graphics are **capital letters**, **line length**, **bold face print**, and **italics**. The use of capital letters, bold face print, and italics generally signal emphasis. Line length helps you to understand the rhythm of a poem. Most poets also use capital letters at the beginning of each poetic line.

Practice 5: Graphics

Read the poem, and answer the questions.

1. How does the use of capitalized words contribute to the way one reads this portion of James Weldon Johnson's poem, "The Teacher"?

> I teach them KNOWLEDGE, but I know
>
> How faint they flicker and how low
>
> The candles of my knowledge glow.
>
> I teach them POWER to will and do,
>
> But only now to learn anew
>
> My own great weakness through and through.
>
> I teach them LOVE for all mankind
>
> And all God's creatures, but I find
>
> My love comes lagging far behind.

2. Read aloud the poem "Life" by Emily Dickinson. Notice how line length affects the rhythm as you read.

> Our share of night to bear,
> Our share of morning,
> Our blank in bliss to fill,
> Our blank in scorning.
>
> Here a star, and there a star,
> Some lose their way.
> Here a mist, and there a mist,
> Afterwards—day!

CHAPTER 9 SUMMARY

Tone

Tone is the attitude that a writer takes toward the audience, a subject, or a character. Writers convey tone through **word choice**, **sentence structure**, **punctuation**, **rhythm**, **repetition**, and **rhyme**.

Sound Devices

Alliteration

Alliteration, is the repetition of consonant sounds at the beginning of words.

Onomatopoeia

Onomatopoeia the use of words whose sounds suggest their meanings. Examples are *boom, swish*, and *tick*.

Rhyme Scheme

Rhyme is the repetition of sounds at the end of words. There are many variations of rhyme schemes. Rhymes that occur at the end of a line are called **end rhymes**. Rhymes within a line are called **internal rhymes**.

Graphics

Sometimes, poets use **graphics**, or details that a reader can see to add special emphasis for reading. Some commonly used poetic graphics are **capital letters**, **line length**, **bold face print**, and **italics**.

CHAPTER 9 REVIEW

Read the poems, and answer the questions that follow.

I Heard a Fly Buzz When I Died

by Emily Dickinson

1 I heard a fly buzz when I died;
2 The stillness round my form
3 Was like the stillness in the air
4 Between the heaves of storm.

5 The eyes beside had wrung them dry,
6 And breaths were gathering sure
7 For that last onset, when the king
8 Be witnessed in his power.

9 I willed my keepsakes, signed away
10 What portion of me I
11 Could make assignable, and then
12 There interposed a fly,

13 With blue, uncertain, stumbling buzz,
14 Between the light and me;
15 And then the windows failed, and then
16 I could not see to see.

1. Which line contains an example of onomatopoeia?

   A. 1   **B.** 3   **C.** 12   **D.** 16

2. Which line pairs use end rhyme?

   A. lines 13 and 15   **C.** lines 2 and 4

   B. lines 10 and 12   **D.** both B and C

3. Which of the following is the rhyme scheme pattern of the poem's first stanza?

   A. abcd   **B.** abab   **C.** abba   **D.** abcb

4. Which of the following lines contains internal rhyme?

   A. line 5   **B.** line 7   **C.** line 10   **D.** none of these

5. Which of the following graphic devices is **not** used in the last stanza?

   A. capital letters   **C.** italics

   B. variation of line length   **D.** none of these

Read the sections from poems below. Then answer the questions that follow each one.

1 The ship was cheered, the harbour cleared,
2 Merrily did we drop
3 Below the kirk, below the hill,
4 Below the light-house top.

–from "The Rime of the Ancient Mariner"
by Samuel Coleridge

6. In this section of the poem, which line contains an internal rhyme?

   A. line 1   **B.** line 2   **C.** line 3   **D.** line 4

7. What is the rhyme scheme of this stanza?

   A. abab   **B.** abcb   **C.** abba   **D.** abcd

8. Which line contains an example of alliteration?

   A. line 1   **B.** line 2   **C.** line 3   **D.** line 4

1 How sweet is the shepherd's sweet lot!
2 From the morn to the evening he strays;
3 He shall follow his sheep all the day,
4 And his tongue shall be filled with praise.

–from William Blake's "Shepherd"

9. Which line contains an example of alliteration?

   A. line 1   **B.** line 2   **C.** line 3   **D.** line 4

1 When my mother died I was very young,

2 And my father sold me while yet my tongue

3 Could scarcely cry 'Weep! weep! weep! weep!'

4 So your chimneys I sweep, and in soot I sleep.

–from William Blake's "The Chimney Sweeper"

10. Which line contains an example of onomatopoeia?

   A. line 1   **B.** line 2   **C.** line 3   **D.** line 4

Now Rann the Kite brings home the night

That Mang the Bat sets free—

The herds are shut in byre and hut

For loosed till dawn are we.

This is the hour of pride and power,

Talon and tush and claw.

Oh, hear the call!—Good hunting all

That keep the Jungle Law!

Night-Song in the Jungle

–from *The Jungle Book* by Rudyard Kipling

11. Which of the following **best** describes the tone of this poem?

    A. scared   **B.** humorous   **C.** angry   **D.** proud

FROM all the jails the boys and girls
   Ecstatically leap, —
Beloved, only afternoon
   That prison doesn't keep.

They storm the earth and stun the air,
   A mob of solid bliss.
Alas! that frowns could lie in wait
   For such a foe as this!

–Emily Dickinson

12. Which of the following **best** describes the speaker's tone in this poem?

    A. celebratory   **B.** disgusted   **C.** intelligent   **D.** hopeful

Chapter 10
Vocabulary

This chapter addresses the following Georgia Performance Standards for reading:

ELA6R2	The student understands and acquires new vocabulary and uses it correctly in reading and writing. The student:
	a. Determines the meaning of unfamiliar words by using word, sentence, and paragraph clues.
	b. Uses knowledge of Greek and Latin affixes to understand unfamiliar vocabulary.
	c. Identifies and interprets words with multiple meanings.
ELA6RC3	The student acquires new vocabulary in each content area and uses it correctly. The student:
	a. Demonstrates an understanding of contextual vocabulary in various subjects.
ELA6RC4	The student establishes a context for information acquired by reading across subject areas. The student:
	c. Determines strategies for finding content and contextual meaning for unfamiliar words and concepts.

Passages, books, stories, and articles that we read are made up of thousands of words. Sometimes, you are very familiar with the words that you see. At other times, you may come across words you don't know. Often you will find at least one or two unfamiliar words when reading. What do you do when you see a word that you do not know? Do you panic? Do you skip over it? Do you decide that the reading selection is too hard and move on to something else? What if the word that you don't know is a part of a reading assignment in your textbook? What if it is something you have to read?

As a student, you know that you have such resources as glossaries and dictionaries to help you with new words. However, when taking a test, you can't always use these resources. This chapter is about building vocabulary skills. After reading this chapter, you will have learned some vocabulary strategies that will help you to be a stronger reader. Let's begin with a look at how to use context clues to find the meaning of unfamiliar words.

CONTEXT CLUES

Often, when you read a literary passage, you see words that you do not know. Even if you are a strong reader, it is still possible to stumble across words that are new to you. When this happens, there are some strategies that you can use to help you figure out the meaning of these words.

When you find unfamiliar words in a passage, one strategy to determine word meaning is using **context clues**. Context clues are words, phrases, and ideas around a word. The context helps to create the meaning of a word. It can also help you find the meaning of words you don't know. For example, what context clues can you find in the following passage?

> Margie entered the house with a sigh, throwing her books to the floor. She had been through three tests and one of Mr. Miltons's boring history lectures—what a *grueling* day!

Perhaps the word *grueling* is new to you. However, there are clues in the passage that might help you come up with a meaning for the word. What are some of these clues? For one, Margie enters the house with a sigh. When do people sigh? When they are happy, sad, angry, tired? Generally, people sigh when they are sad, tired, or frustrated. Reading on, we note that Margie has had a day full of tests and lectures. It would be safe to say that she is most likely feeling tired. Given these context clues, which of the following is the most likely meaning of the word *grueling*?

    A. lovely

    B. exhausting

    C. funny

    D. depressing

If you chose B, *exhausting*, you are correct! Using clues from the passage, you were able to figure out the meaning of the word. When taking a test, you will need to quickly go through a mental process:

- Look for clues in the sentence or passage.
- Narrow your choices according to the context clues you find.

Also try replacing the word you don't know with each of the possible answers to see which one seems to fit best.

Practice 1: Context Clues

Read the following passage. Answer the questions that follow the passage.

In the mythical village of Hith, the eldest *sage* was named Jantus. Jantus was the one that village members consulted in the time of crisis. He was there to solve everyone's problems and offer sound advice. Jantus' wisdom was very greatly respected, so much so, that village dwellers from even the most *remote* areas of Hith would come from far and wide to seek his advice.

Now, Jantus was slow-moving in his old age. He had learned through time and experience that it was more *profitable* for one to take his time about things and make a wise decision, than to rush head on into the fate of failure. It was his daily *ritual* to rise early. One day, as Jantus sat in his hut, *pondering* over the work of the day, he heard a strange noise in the distance…

1. The word *sage* **most likely** means

    A. an elder.

    B. a man.

    C. a wise person.

    D. a strong person.

2. The word *remote* **most likely** means

    A. far away.

    B. nearby.

    C. in a neighboring village.

    D. neither far or near.

3. The word *profitable* **most likely** means

    A. smart.   **B.** offensive.   **C.** selfish.   **D.** valuable.

4. The word *ritual* most likely means

    A. a good idea.

    B. a guiding path.

    C. an established routine.

    D. an embarrassing moment.

5. The word *pondering* **most likely** means

    A. thinking about something.

    B. talking about something.

    C. imagining a solution.

    D. solving a puzzle.

SYNONYMS AND ANTONYMS

Many English words have similar and opposite meanings of one another. Words that have the same meaning as other words are called **synonyms**. Words with opposite meanings of other words are called **antonyms**. Here are some examples of synonym and antonym pairs.

Synonyms	Antonyms
great, fabulous	young, old
tiny, small	cheap, expensive
large, big	tall, short
angry, mad	dirty, clean
noisy, loud	shiny, dull

Practice 2:   Synonyms and Antonyms

For each of the following, choose the **synonym** for the italicized word.

1. The *mischievous* puppy got into everything.

    A. naughty   **B.** angry   **C.** dirty   **D.** sleepy

2. The *tenant* in apartment C always paid his rent on time.

    A. lady   **B.** man   **C.** renter   **D.** elder

3. In some places, frog legs are a great *delicacy*.

    A. treat   **B.** lace   **C.** price   **D.** trouble

4. *Invariably,* whenever Justin didn't study for his science quizzes, he got poor scores.

    A. angrily   **B.** unfortunately   **C.** consistently   **D.** luckily

5. The *gaunt* stranger looked as if he hadn't eaten in days.

    A. bony   **B.** tall   **C.** shy   **D.** tired

WORD MEANING ACROSS SUBJECTS

Sometimes in your reading, you will see words that are familiar to you from other school subjects. Being familiar with these words from your classes will help you be a better reader overall. Your familiarity with these words may also help you to identify the meaning of new words. Also, as a reading strategy, you will want to use context clues to help you with the meaning of words that are unfamiliar. Remember that context clues are details in writing that help you to understand words based on how they are used.

Take, for example, the word *perimeter*. In math, you have probably learned that *perimeter* means the distance around something. For example, you might be given a drawing of a square that is four inches on each side. If the teacher asks you to find the perimeter of the square, you should come up with 16 inches. 4+4+4+4=16. Imagine that you are reading a fiction story and you see the following phrase:

> Foaming and grunting, the angry dog paced paced around and
> around the perimeter of the fenced yard.

What do you think the sentence means? It means that the dog walked along the fence that enclosed entire the yard. Let's try a few more for practice.

Practice 3: Word Meaning across Subjects

1. On the long trip to Grandma's house, Ellie was able to use her *solar* calculator to complete her math homework. A solar calculator is one that is

    A. very large.   **C.** powered by batteries.

    B. powered by the sun.   **D.** none of the above.

2. A school that is filled with gangs and violence does not make a good learning *environment* for any student. The term environment here means

    A. surroundings or conditions.   **C.** ecology.

    B. a planet's ecosystem.   **D.** the food chain.

3. In language arts, Anna's teacher gave them a *formula* for writing paragraphs. The term formula here means:

    A. a mathematical equation.   **C.** a form of writing.

    B. a systematic format.   **D.** none of these.

WORDS WITH MULTIPLE MEANINGS

Sometimes in your reading you will come across **homographs**—words that are spelled alike but have **multiple meanings**. These words have a clear definition in one context and another definition when used in a different context. When you come across words with multiple meanings, you need to decide which definition of the word best fits with the sentence. Take a look at the following example:

> In the *remote* forests of Hith, there lived strange and terrible creatures.

> Planning to change the television channel, Dhruti reached for the *remote*.

In the first sentence, the word *remote* is an adjective that means "far away." In the next sentence, the word *remote* is the "device used to change television channels." Can you think of other examples of words that have multiple meanings?

Practice 4:   Words with Multiple Meanings

Read each set of sentences, and answer the questions that follow.

1. Which use of the word *waste* is a verb that means "to use unwisely"?

    A. Teachers advise students not to *waste* class time.

    B. Throw that *waste* in the garbage can.

2. Which use of the word *scale(s)* means "an instrument used for measurement"?

    A. Harrison placed the bananas on the produce *scale*.

    B. As Julie's mother cleaned the fish, Julie marveled at the texture of the *scales*.

3. Which use of the word *band* means "a simple un-grooved ring"?

    A. Harry booked a popular *band* for the spring party.

    B. Mrs. Wallace regretted losing her precious wedding *band*.

4. Which use of the word *bow* means "to bend forward at the waist as a gesture of respect"?

    A. The young gentleman took a *bow* before the princess.

    B. The dog shook vigorously enough to loosen the *bow* around its neck.

GREEK AND LATIN ROOTS AND AFFIXES

Many words in the English language come from Greek and Latin. This is good news for you as a reader. By being familiar with Greek and Latin roots and affixes, you can determine the meanings of some unfamiliar words.

Roots and **affixes** (**prefixes** and **suffixes**) are the building blocks of words. A root is a basic part of a word that sometimes can stand alone; it can have one or more affixes attached to it to form other words.

> **Example:** The root *cent* can stand alone; it means "a penny."
> *Cent* means "one hundred," and there are 100 pennies in a dollar.

A prefix is a letter or several letters added to the front of a word to form a new word. When a prefix is added, the word changes meaning.

> **Example:** When you add the prefix *per* to the root *cent*, you get the new word *percent*. It means "part of 100." If you have 50 percent of something, it means you have half of it (because 50 is half of 100).

A suffix is a letter or several letters added to the end of a word to form a new word.

> **Example:** Adding *-age* to the end of percent forms the word *percentage*. Since *-age* means "doing, being," the new word means "being a part of 100," as in the sentence, "Only a small percentage of students at my school uses a cell phone."

COMMONLY USED GREEK AND LATIN ROOTS AND AFFIXES

Take a look at the **roots**, **prefixes**, and **suffixes** in these tables. If you don't know some of the example words, look them up in a dictionary.

Root Word	Meaning	Example
aqua	water	aquatic
biblio, bibl	book	biblical
bio	life	biology
cent	one hundred	centimeter
dent, odon	tooth	dentist
derm	skin	dermatologist
dic, dict	say, speak	dictionary

Prefix	Meaning	Example
ant, anti	against	antonym
auto	self	autobiography
bi	two	bicycle
ben, bon	good	benefit
co, con.corn	together	conform
extra	beyond	extraterrestrial
hyper	above, beyond	hyperspace
kilo	thousand	kilowatt
mal	bad	malicious
micro	small	microscope
migr	move, travel	migrant
multi	many, much	multiple
ob, op	against, toward	obstruct, oppose
omni	all	omnidirectional
per	through	perfect
pre	before	preschool
post	after	postpone
pseudo	false, counterfeit	pseudonym
retro	back, behind	retrofit
semi	half	semimonthly
tele	far off	telescope
trans	over, across	transport
tri	three	tripod
un	not	undo
uni	one	universe

Suffix	Meaning	Example
able	capable of being	teachable
age	doing, being	marriage
ance	state of being	brilliance
ary	relating to, like	contrary
ence	state, fact, quality	difference
ic	like, nature of	metallic
ion, tion, ation	being, the result of	starvation
ism	act, condition	realism
ist	one who	artist
ive	of, quality of	active
ment	a means, act, or state	advancement
or	condition of	horror
ory	place for	rectory
ous	characterized by	nervous
ize	to become like	fossilize

Practice 5:   Greek and Latin Roots, Prefixes, and Suffixes

Use the list of Greek and Latin roots and affixes to help you answer the following questions.

1. An *omniscient* narrator

    A. knows the thoughts, feelings, and motivations of all characters.

    B. knows the thoughts, feelings, and motivations of some characters.

    C. is a character in the story.

    D. none of these

2. A _____ has only one wheel.

    A. unicycle   **B.** bicycle   **C.** tricycle   **D.** none of these

3. The word *diction* refers to the way someone _____ .

    A. eats   **B.** speaks   **C.** thinks   **D.** walks

4. How many meters are there in a *kilometer*?

    A. 100   **B.** 500   **C.** 1,000   **D.** 10,000

5. *Biology* is the study of _____ .

    A. the stars   **B.** life   **C.** the earth   **D.** physics

VOCABULARY IN VARIOUS SUBJECTS

Another important skill is being able to **understand vocabulary in different subjects** in school. This means that you should be able to read and understand words in all of your academic subjects—language arts, math, science, and social studies.

In this section, we will focus on science and social studies. Science and social studies textbooks are filled with many informational passages. They contain important terminology (words specific to a subject). As you study theses subjects, you will need to pay very close attention to the important words. Learning words in a content area will greatly help your understanding of the topics covered.

Reading your science or social studies texts, you will encounter words that you don't know. Generally, if the words are technical and relate specifically to the subject of the text, then you will be able to look in your book's glossary for help. The glossary is an important tool that a good reader uses to help understand the text. Sometimes, though, there is no glossary. You can use the vocabulary strategies in this chapter to figure out words in any subject!

Practice 6: Vocabulary in Various Subjects

Read the passages, and answer the questions that follow.

Through *seismology*, we have learned a great deal about the *natural phenomenon* known as the earthquake. When *seismic waves* pass through the earth, the result is an earthquake. During an earthquake, the earth shakes. In addition to causing a great deal of fear and superstition, damage as the result of earthquakes has caused some of the most horrendous tragedies known to humanity. Scientists now know that earthquakes are most likely to occur along *geologic* faults.

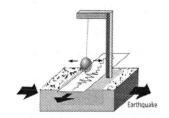

1. From the passage, the reader learns that the term *seismic wave* means

    A. shocks of electricity that occur underground.

    B. strong bursts of water that ripple across the ocean and onto the shore.

    C. movement produced when stored energy in the Earth's crust is suddenly released.

    D. none of these

2. From clues in the passage, the reader can infer that *seismology* is

    A. the science that studies natural phenomena.

    B. the science that studies rocks.

    C. the science that studies earthquakes.

    D. the science that studies volcanoes.

3. The meaning of *natural phenomenon* is

   A. an unusual pattern in weather.

   B. an observable event in nature.

   C. an earthquake.

   D. seismology.

4. The term *geologic* refers to

   A. things having to do with the study of earthquakes.

   B. things having to do with the study of seismic waves.

   C. things having to do with the study of the earth's structure.

   D. none of these

CHAPTER 10 SUMMARY

Context clues are words, phrases, or ideas in a sentence that surround a word and help to create its meaning in the sentence.

Words that have the same meaning as other words are called **synonyms**. Words with opposite meanings of other words are called **antonyms**.

Many words have **multiple meanings**. As you read, pay attention to how words are used in a sentence to help determine which meaning is intended. Also, use the idea of sentence sense to help rule out any meanings that are unlikely. Also pay attention to the word's part of speech in a sentence.

In the English language, many words with which we are familiar have their origins in Greek and Latin. By being familiar with common **Greek and Latin roots and affixes**, you will be better able to determine the meaning of unknown words.

Another important vocabulary skill is being able to **read across the academic curriculum**. This means that you should be able to read and comprehend words in all of your academic subjects—language arts, math, science, and social studies. Pay attention to how words are used. Employ the tools of your textbook, such as the glossary and footnotes, to decipher technical vocabulary.

CHAPTER 10 REVIEW

Read the passage, and answer the questions that follow.

Charlie was a kid with big dreams. He wasn't the type of kid who was satisfied with one or two big ideas. Oh, no—Charlie had many *aspirations*.

1. Based upon its use in context, the word *aspirations* **most likely** means

    A. asthma.　　**B.** things to do.　　**C.** brains.　　**D.** dreams.

Eugene looked down at his desk. The algebraic equations may as well have been the words and symbols of a foreign language. Suddenly, it was as if the numbers and lines of his test's equations danced off the paper and romped across his desk in a cruel *taunt*. It was as if the elements of the equation in front of him were mocking him for his ignorance.

2. Which word is **most** similar to the word *taunt*?

    A. stare　　**B.** tease　　**C.** gesture　　**D.** remark

Most people do not have the ability to predict events that will occur in the future. Rather, most people are content to experience each day as it occurs. In ancient times, some people consulted *soothsayers* for predictions of future events and other advice.

3. Which of the following **most likely** defines the term *soothsayer*?

    A. a person who cleans and repairs teeth

    B. a person who talks constantly

    C. a person who professes to predict the future

    D. a person who is wise or intelligent

For items 4 and 5, choose the best *synonym* for the italicized word.

4. That night, as Khumar sat down to dinner with his family, his eyes wandered *jealously* toward the gold medal that hung around his younger brother's neck.

    A. enviously　　**B.** angrily　　**C.** eagerly　　**D.** anxiously

5. Choose the **synonym** for the italicized word in this sentence.

> Still in the beginner's group, Marlin was not exactly a *proficient* swimmer.

   A. efficient   **B.** competent   **C.** elegant   **D.** destined

For items 7 and 8, choose the best *antonym* for the italicized word.

6. There was a *feast* in the great land of Hoyat.

   A. festival   **B.** depression   **C.** famine   **D.** banquet

7. I did not pay because the caterers served *unsavory* food.

   A. delicious   **B.** saved   **C.** chunky   **D.** cold

8. What is **most likely** the meaning of the word *unidentifiable*?

   A. not able to be identified   **C.** already identified

   B. no time to identify   **D.** one of a kind

9. What is **most likely** the meaning of the word *benefactor*?

   A. a kindly helper who gives aid

   B. a person whose joints are very flexible

   C. someone who is familiar with many facts

   D. a father with many children

10. What is **most likely** the meaning of the word *dermatology*?

   A. the study of light   **C.** the study of skin

   B. the study of civilizations   **D.** the study of chemicals

11. How many wheels does a *tricycle* have?

  A. one   **B.** two   **C.** three   **D.** four

12. In which of the following sentences is the word *rose* a past tense form of the verb *to rise*, meaning "to assume an upright position"?

  A. Sharon *rose* from the sofa to answer the ringing doorbell.

  B. The *rose* was the only decorative item in the unfurnished office.

13. In which of the following sentences does the word *bank* mean a place of financial business?

  A. Dustin rushed to the *bank* to make his deposit.

  B. The boy and his dog spend lazy summer days lying by the river *bank*.

14. What is **most likely** the meaning of the word *utopia*?

  A. an ideal society   **C.** a dark place

  B. a dirty place   **D.** a pretty society

15. What is **most likely** the meaning of the term *extraterrestrial life*?

  A. life after death   **C.** the life of elderly people

  B. life beyond Earth   **D.** traveling outside the country

16. After gathering *data* from her classmates, Jenna had all of the information she needed to make a campaign speech for student council. The term "data" here means

  A. information.   **B.** votes.   **C.** advice.   **D.** none of these.

17. Lindsey watched from the backseat as her father entered the *coordinates* for their trip into the car's GPS. The term coordinates here means

  A. things that match or can be worn together.

  B. channels.

  C. destination points.

  D. none of these

GA 6th Grade CRCT Reading Practice Test 1

The purpose of this practice test is to measure your knowledge in reading comprehension. This practice test is based on the GPS-based CRCT standards for reading and adheres to the sample question format provided by the Georgia Department of Education.

General Directions:

1. Read all directions carefully.

2. Read each question or sample. Then choose the best answer.

3. Choose only one answer for each question. If you change an answer, be sure to erase your original answer completely.

Community Learning Day

Flanders will hold its first Community Learning Day this Saturday. This is your chance to meet your neighbors, have fun, and learn something new. All classes take place at the community center. The program directors advise everyone to register for classes by email. Class enrollment is free but limited. At 8 a.m., the lobby of the community center will be open. People can sign up in person at this time for classes not yet filled.

Learners of all ages must check-in at 9 a.m. at the welcome desk. Be prepared to show proof of town residency at this time. All students will receive class entrance passes at check-in. Children under the age of eighteen must sign-up with a parent.

Classes begin at 9:15 a.m. Please do not be late. Volunteers will serve lunch at noon in the tent. The directors ask that everyone return to the lobby after the last class. Fill out the end survey and let us know how we did with this program. This will also be a chance to suggest classes for the next Community Learning Day.

There will also be a sign-up sheet for teachers for the next Community Day. All teachers are volunteers. Please consider sharing your talents with the community.

9:15–10:45 a.m.
Parent and Child Yoga
Learn How to Play Bridge
Planning a Budget
Plant an Herb Garden
Basics of Grouting

11:00–Noon
Power Walking
Basics of Chess
The Perfect Bow
Shuffleboard
Choosing the Right Tool for the Job

1:00–3:00 p.m.
Chocolate, Chocolate, Chocolate!
Build a Garden Bench
Country Line Dancing
Folk Painting Basics
Painting Pictures with Words

3:00–5:00 p.m.
Shake, Rattle, and Roll!
Volleyball
Basket Weaving
Basic Home Repairs
Tai Chi

1. The article is organized in   ELA6R1.c
   A. problem and solution order.
   B. cause and effect order.
   C. spatial order.
   D. time order.

2. According to the schedule,   ELA6R1.b
   at what time can you learn
   how to power walk?

   A. 9:15   C. 1:00
   B. 11:00   D. 3:00

3. What was the author's   ELA6RC2.e
   purpose in writing the
   article?
   A. to persuade people to exercise
   B. to inform people about the
      activities
   C. to explain how to play shuffleboard
   D. to describe the new community
      center

4. In paragraph 1, the word   ELA6R2.a
   register means
   A. to record like a reflex.
   B. to get special protection.
   C. to sing in a set range of notes.
   D. to formally add a name to a list.

5. What is the **main** idea of the   ELA6R1.d
   article?
   A. Many different classes will be
      offered on Community Learning
      Day.
   B. Volunteers are needed to teach
      classes and serve lunch.
   C. Everyone must prove they live in
      town before taking any of the
      classes.
   D. Children may not take classes
      without their parents.

6. The article would **most**   ELA6RC2.d
   likely appear in
   A. an encyclopedia.
   B. a state tour guide.
   C. a local newspaper.
   D. a national magazine.

Excerpt from *The New Year*

by Florence Henrietta Darwin

Characters

STEVE BROWNING, a Blacksmith, also Parish Clerk.

JANE BROWNING.

DORRY BROWNING, aged twelve.

ACT II.—Scene 1.

The living room in the Brownings' cottage. The room is divided by a curtain which screens the fireside end from the draught of the principal door. To the right of the fireplace is a door leading upstairs. Chairs are grouped round the hearth, and there is a table at which JANE BROWNING is ironing a dress by the light of one candle. DORRY leans against the table, watching her.

JANE. [Putting aside the iron.] There, you take and lay it on the bed upstairs, and mind you does it careful, for I'm not a-going to iron it twice.

[She lays the dress carefully across DORRY'S arms.]

DORRY. Don't the lace look nice, Gran'ma?

JANE. You get along upstairs and do as I says, and then come straight down again.

DORRY. Couldn't I put it on once, Gran'ma, just to see how it do look on me?

JANE. And get it all creased up afore to-morrow! Whatever next! You go and lay it on the bed this minute, do you hear?

DORRY. [Leaving the room by the door to the right.] I'd like to put it on just once, I would.

[JANE BROWNING blows out the candle and puts away the iron and ironing cloth. She stirs up the fire and then sits down by it as DORRY comes back.]

DORRY. Dad's cleaning of himself ever so—I heard the water splashing something dreadful as I went by his door.

JANE. 'Tis a-smartening of hisself up for this here dancing as he be about, I reckon.

DORRY. [Sitting down on a stool.] I'd like to go along, too, and see the dancing up at the schools to-night, I would.

JANE. And what next, I should like to know!

DORRY. And wear my new frock what's ironed, and the beads what Miss Sims gave me.

JANE. [Looking out at the window.] I'm thinking as we shall get some snow by and by. 'Tis come over so dark all of a sudden.

DORRY. Couldn't I go along of they, Gran'ma, and wear my new frock, and the beads, too? I never see'd them dance th' old year out yet, I haven't.

JANE. Get along with you, Dorry. 'Tis many a year afore you'll be of an age for such foolishness. And that's what I calls it, this messing about with dancing and music and I don't know what.

7. Who is the protagonist in this act?   ELA6R1.e.iii

   A. Steve Browning

   B. Jane Brownings

   C. Dorry Browning

   D. It is difficult to tell from this brief scene.

8. The reader learns about Dorry and Jane's relationship through   ELA6R1.b.iii

   A. the use of dialogue.

   B. the list of characters.

   C. the use of description.

   D. the voice of a narrator.

9. The author uses *italics* to   ELA6R1.h.iii

   A. show the narrator's part in the play.

   B. separate the setting from the dialogue.

   C. describe the relationship of the characters.

   D. emphasize the important events in this act.

10. Which strategy would be **most** helpful for determining the meaning of the word *frock* in the act?   ELA6RC4.c

   A. list and review the major points in the act

   B. preview the text to locate all unknown words

   C. reread the material and write down all context clues you find

   D. access prior knowledge of what a girl would wear during that time

11. What is the plot of the act?   ELA6R1.e.iii

   A. Dad wants to look good for the dance.

   B. Jane wants Dorry to learn how to iron.

   C. Grandma does not like to listen to music.

   D. Dorry wants to dress up and go to the dance.

12. The setting of the act can **best** be described as   ELA6R1.e.iii

   A. a cottage long ago

   B. a school long ago

   C. a cottage in modern times

   D. a school in modern times

The Lady of the Press

(1) Ink may have always flowed through Sarah Hillhouse's veins. However, in the late 1700s, no one would have guessed she would become the editor of a newspaper. At that time, most women worked only in the home. Sarah Hillhouse was not like most women of her time.

(2) The United States was growing. The government needed people to move to unsettled parts of the country. The government passed homesteading laws. Under these laws, people could move onto free lands. If they settled on the land, the head of the household received the land for free. The government began granting homesteads in Georgia. Sarah and her husband, David, answered the call for help and headed south. Sarah was born and raised in the Northeast. She had never lived far from her family. Moving to Georgia meant leaving them behind. It even meant leaving their daughters for awhile.

(3) In 1786, Sarah and David moved to Washington. It was a small town on the Georgia frontier. David opened a general store there. Sarah predicted he would be successful. Sarah must have missed her family. Life in Georgia was very different from the life Sarah knew back East. The frontier was a rough-and-tumble place. Sarah could not be convinced to bring "my dear little lambs in this flock of wolves, as I may properly call many of the inhabitants of this state!" Before long though, she met many new people. Sarah began to see the town was not as uncivilized as she had first thought. She began to see it as her home.

(4) The town had a local newspaper. In 1801, David decided to buy it. He changed the name of the paper and became the publisher. David ran the printing presses and Sarah ran their home.

(5) Two years later Sarah became a widow. She was only forty years old, and there was another baby on the way. With David gone, Sarah had a hard decision to make. Did she uproot her family and move back to the Northeast? Did she stay in Georgia and raise her family on her own? The answer made Sarah a part of Georgia history. In 1803, she took over the newspaper. She became the first female editor in the state.

(6) Sarah went straight to work. She learned how the printing presses worked. She learned how to manage a business. She worked to make the newspaper more useful to its readers. By including articles about other parts of the country, she helped the local people learn about places they had never visited. She helped the business grow by printing items for other people and selling blank paper and forms. She did all of this while making sure that her home ran smoothly.

(7) Running a home and a business was hard work. Sarah showed people that a woman could be strong enough and smart enough to do both.

13. Which is the **best** concluding sentence for the article?   ELA6R1.a

   A. Throughout history, women have worked hard to achieve their goals.

   B. Sarah probably always missed her family and her home in the North-east.

   C. Today, many women work as writers, editors, and publishers of newspapers.

   D. Today, her example continues to inspire women to try new things and do their best.

14. The article is organized in   ELA6R1.c

   A. time order.

   B. spatial order.

   C. cause and effect order.

   D. problem and solution order.

15. What is the main idea of paragraph 5?   ELA6R1.d

   A. Sarah became a widow.

   B. Sarah was having a baby.

   C. Sarah was forty years old.

   D. Sarah had a choice to make.

16. What detail from the article supports the author's statement that "Sarah was not like most women of her time"?   ELA6R1.d

   A. Sarah predicted he would be successful.

   B. Sarah must have missed her family.

   C. Two years later Sarah became a widow.

   D. She learned how the printing presses worked.

17. What was the author's purpose in writing the article?   ELA6RC2.e

   A. to explain homesteading

   B. to encourage people to write

   C. to inform people about Sarah Hillhouse

   D. to tell a fun story about pioneer women

18. If *pre-* means "before" and *dic* means "speak," which word means "said in advance of an event"?   ELA6R2.b

   A. diction

   B. dictated

   C. predicted

   D. prescribed

Exploring a Cave

(1) Keisha directed the beam of her flashlight upward. The ceiling of the cave, hundreds of feet above, was dressed in shadows. She heard the faint rustle of bat wings as the bats flew into the shadows. Although she knew the bats were her hosts, she was glad she could not see them. Keisha tugged on Tamarr's jacket sleeve and whispered, "We're not alone here."

(2) Keisha continued to scan her surroundings. The ceiling dipped in the uneven corners of the cave. The shallow crevices looked like a jungle of rock icicles. Colorful crystals had formed on the taller cave walls, giving them a shimmery appearance. She remembered reading in her science book that both of these sights were caused by water dripping from the walls and ceiling.

(3) The sound of water dripping into a wading pool caused Keisha to try and view the cave as a whole instead of its parts. When she found the source of the sound, she nudged Tamarr and pointed. A thin trail of water trickled along the cave floor, twisting and turning around the rocks. Keisha hoped she would later see where the trail ended. She pictured it growing into an underground river. The tour guide's voice interrupted her thoughts. "I'm going to turn the lights on now," he said. "It may take your eyes a minute to adjust to the light, so everyone should stay where they are now."

(4) The lights flashed on, and Keisha squinted as she took another look around the cave. The cave was a work of art. Although she could see everything much more clearly in the light, she preferred the peacefulness of the dark cave.

---

19. The story is told from the point of view of   ELA6R1.f

   A. Keisha

   B. Tamarr

   C. the tour guide

   D. an unknown narrator

20. The author uses alliteration in paragraph 3 to help the reader   ELA6R1.h.i

   A. read the passage more quickly.

   B. see and hear the flow of the water.

   C. know why Keisha looks for the water.

   D. understand how crystals form in a cave.

21. What **most** likely is the purpose of the dialogue in the story?   ELA6R1.b

   A. to describe the setting of the story

   B. to explain the conflict in the story

   C. to show how other people see Keisha

   D. to show that Keisha is not alone in the cave

22. Which sentence contains a metaphor?   ELA6R1.a

   A. The ceiling of the cave, hundreds of feet above, was dressed in shadows.

   B. She heard the faint rustle of bat wings as the bats flew into the shadows.

   C. Although she knew the bats were her hosts, she was glad she could not see them.

   D. Keisha tugged on Tamarr's jacket sleeve and whispered, "We're not alone here."

Toes

(1) Trapped inside a wooly web,
Beneath a leather den,
Are found a group of captives.
Let's call them One through Ten.

(2) Denied their right to freedom,
To scrunch happily in sand,
Number One appealed to the others,
Let's wriggle till we touch land.

(3) He soon was joined in his struggle,
By Number Two and Number Three.
They called out to the others,
Let's wriggle till we're free!

(4) They wriggled and they wiggled;
They fought a valiant fight.
Number Four, Five, and Six join in,
Let's wriggle for what's right!

(5) Now the six fought bravely,
To set their comrades free.
They shed their woolen shackles.
Let's wriggle as a family!

(6) The ten prisoners bound by goal,
Worked at their fastest pace,
Let's wriggle all together,
Or it's failure we will face!

(7) As daring as these digits were,
They needed outside help.
So clever Number Eight said,
"Let's wriggle till he yelps!"

(8) Off came the leather casing,
And the torn woolen boundary.
Ten toes had been paroled,
Free to wriggle in sand and sea!

23. What is the main theme of   ELA6R1.d
    the poem?

    A. Nothing in life is completely free.

    B. Anything is possible with team-work.

    C. True happiness comes from within.

    D. Walk a mile in another person's shoes.

24. Stanza 7 is an example of   ELA6R1.h.ii

    A. metaphor.

    B. simile.

    C. personification.

    D. internal rhyme.

25. Which homonym **correctly**   ELA6R2.c
    completes both spaces in
    the following sentence?

Your toes will _____ a complaint, if you kick the fence _____.

    A. gate   C. shout

    B. post   D. lodge

26. Which word **best** describes   ELA6R1.e
    the toes?

    A. silent

    B. divided

    C. frightened

    D. determined

JOAN SMITH FOR MAYOR!

Elect JOAN SMITH Mayor
Your vote can make a difference!

HOME
BIOGRAPHY
EXPERIENCE
PLANS
A NEW
FOX HOLLOW
CAMPAIGN
SCHEDULE
SUPPORT
CONTACT
PHOTO
ALBUM

Are you tired of dodging potholes on Main Street? Your vote can make a difference. Have you been inconvenienced by lengthy waits for construction inspections? Your vote can make a difference. Are you angry because our mayor cut garbage and recycling collections in half? Your vote can make a difference.

Responsible citizens of Fox Hollow have seen too many town services shrink or disappear all together. Where is the dog park that Mayor Jones promised voters in the last election? Why are our playing fields still overbooked? Where is the funding for new library books? Concerned citizens want change. Your vote can make a difference.

Joan Smith is a lifetime resident of Fox Hollow. Like us, she knows what strong leadership can do for this town. Like us, she remembers a time when our leaders cared about both our wallets and our quality of life. And like us, she knows we will never return to that quality of life under our current mayor.

Recently, we talked to shoppers in town. We asked about the current mayor. Not one citizen described Mayor Jones as, "truthful and reliable." Clearly, the hard-working people of Fox Hollow need a change. Your vote can make a difference.

On Tuesday, the caring people of Fox Hollow will cast their ballots for Joan Smith for mayor. If like them, you want a mayor who will make changes now, a mayor who cares about the community, a mayor who knows what changes need to be made, then cast your ballot for Joan Smith. Your vote can make a difference!

> "Joan Smith is very patriotic. She always flies the American flag on Memorial Day."
> – Abby Rose, neighbor.
>
> "Joan was always a responsible child. She never forgot her homework."
> – Doris Burke, third grade teacher

HOME   BIOGRAPHY   EXPERIENCE   PLANS   A NEW FOX HOLLOW   CAMPAIGN SCHEDULE   SUPPORT   CONTACT   PHOTO ALBUM

---

27. Paragraph 3 is an example of a propaganda technique called   ELA6LSV2.a

    A. card stacking.

    B. testimonial.

    C. transfer.

    D. repetition.

28. What information is missing from this Web page?   ELA6LSV2.a

    A. why Joan Smith wants change

    B. when these changes will be made

    C. what changes Joan Smith will make

    D. where Joan Smith wants to make changes

29. The sentence, "Your vote can make a difference," is an example of the technique called   ELA6LSV2.a

    A. glittering generalities.

    B. bandwagon.

    C. repetition.

    D. testimonial.

30. The quotes from people saying things about the candidate are examples of the propaganda technique called   ELA6LSV2.a

    A. bandwagon.

    B. testimonials.

    C. glittering generalities.

    D. unfinished comparisons.

31. Which sentence contains   ELA6LSV2.a
   "loaded words"?

   A. Concerned citizens want change.

   B. Your vote can make a difference.

   C. Recently, we talked to shoppers in town.

   D. We asked about the current mayor.

32. What message is found in   ELA6RC2.a
   this Web page?

   A. Everyone should vote.

   B. Voters come in all ages.

   C. If you care about your town, you will vote for Joan Smith.

   D. If you need help in Fox Hollow, Joan Smith will volunteer.

33. The author **most** likely   ELA6RC2.f
   placed American flags on the Web page to

   A. inform readers that Fox Hollow is in the United States.

   B. persuade readers that voting for Joan Smith is patriotic.

   C. encourage readers to fly the American flag on Election Day.

   D. illustrate that flags are found in and around all voting places.

34. In paragraph 5, the word   ELA6RC3.a
   cast means

   A. to move by throwing.

   B. to assign parts in a play.

   C. to formally deposit a vote.

   D. to mold solids from liquids.

Moving Day

(1) Our adventure began on a crowded Missouri River steamboat. This was the quickest route to Independence, the jumping off point for our journey.

(2) When we reached our destination, we settled our wagon near hundreds of others. Pa let me come along when he went into town to arrange for the necessaries for our trip. The hustle and bustle of the town took my breath away. The streets were bulging with people, mules, and horses. Rows of shops played host to the masses, inviting them in to part with some money. The people responded by scurrying in and out of the stores, their arms full of supplies. Wooden corrals held livestock for sale. I saw a beautiful horse, but Pa said that oxen were more practical for the rough road ahead. The smell of the livestock mixed with the scent of smoke from the blacksmith shops. As we walked, the voices of the emigrants and the owners dickering over the price of the animals drifted down the street. The banging of the blacksmith's hammers shook my insides like the bass drum in the orchestra. It swept me up in its music, and I found myself almost waltzing beside Pa.

(3) Pa had said we would have to wait until the grass was tall enough to feed the animals. Finally, it was time to set off for our new home. We loaded the necessaries Pa had bought in town onto the wagon. Pa lifted the heavy sacks of flour, sugar, and coffee onto the wooden floor. We needed enough food to make it to the nearest fort. Ma and I found room for bandages and medicine. Ma said that we needed to bring them, but she hoped we never used them. Before long, we had filled the wagon. Pa had to hang the pots and pans on the outside of the wagon with the rain barrel and the toolbox. At last the packing was finished, and we were ready for the next leg of our adventure to begin.

(4) There was one last thing for me to do before we left Independence. I hurried over to the rock that had served as my seat while we were there. I had spent many hours sitting there, daydreaming about our new home. I picked up a small stone to use as my pen. I scratched onto the rock, "Sallie Morgan sat here, but left to seek adventure."

(5) Ma settled in the seat next to Pa, and I squeezed in between them. Ma said it was too dangerous for me to walk here, where livestock moved shoulder to shoulder down the road. The road was so crowded our wagon got stuck in a traffic jam at the edge of town. Pa knew how to handle a wagon and team, but some of the men had no experience. Some ran their oxen into trees or tipped their wagons as they tried to maneuver through the crowds. I felt proud of Pa's skills as he kept our wagon steady, despite the deep ruts in the road. There were thousands of miles between us and Oregon, but **we were on our way**!

35. The story relates to the period in United States history known as ELA6R1.c

  A. the Dust Bowl.

  B. the Civil War.

  C. the Great Depression.

  D. Westward Expansion.

36. Why does the author use the word *banging* in paragraph 2? ELA6R1.h.i

  A. to help the reader hear what the narrator hears

  B. to explain to the reader what a blacksmith does

  C. to help the reader know how busy the blacksmith is

  D. to show the reader the town through the narrator's eyes

37. In paragraph 2, "Rows of shops played host to the masses," is an example of ELA6R1.h.ii

  A. simile.

  B. metaphor.

  C. hyperbole.

  D. personification.

38. Which **best** describes the narration of the story? ELA6R1.f

  A. first person through Pa

  B. first person through Sallie

  C. third person limited

  D. third person omniscient

39. Why does the author use descriptive language in paragraph 5? ELA6R1.b

  A. to explain why Sallie is excited about the trip

  B. to show that Pa should lead this wagon train

  C. to show how crowded and dangerous the trail could be

  D. to explain why so few people traveled on the Oregon Trail

40. Which is a theme of the story? ELA6R1.d

  A. Life is an adventure.

  B. Wisdom comes with age.

  C. Bad luck is better than no luck.

  D. Into every life some rain must fall.

41. How is the tone of the story **best** shown? ELA6R1.g

  A. through the list of supplies in paragraph 4

  B. through the punctuation found in paragraph 1

  C. through the use of the words *music* and *waltzing* in paragraph 2

  D. through the rhythm of the rhyming words found in each paragraph

42. What was the effect of the bold print in paragraph 5? ELA6R1.h.iii

  A. It showed readers the story was ending.

  B. It showed readers that Sallie felt excited.

  C. It showed readers the trip was difficult.

  D. It showed readers that Ma felt nervous.

Student Representatives Needed

(1) Would you like to represent your school? Do you have a quick smile and an *outgoing* personality? Do you like meeting and talking with new people? We are looking for a few good people to add to our program. Interested students can pick up an application. The deadline for submitting applications is October 1. The complete *process* is explained below.

(2) Student reps fill an important role. They help welcome new students to our school. A student rep is assigned to each new student. They show the students around the school and help them adjust to their new surroundings. This year the program includes our kindergarten students. The reps will help their student feel "at home" in school.

(3) Responsibilities of student reps go beyond the school walls. They also represent the school at town events, like the Founder's Day Parade. In addition, the students represent our school at events in other schools in the county.

Qualifications include:

- Student must be in grade 6 or higher.

- Student must maintain a B average or better.

- Student should have at least 3 hours a week to devote to the program.

Read the following information carefully. Follow all directions.

Step 1 Pick up an application. Use a ballpoint pen to complete your application. Answer every question. If you are unsure of any question, ask for help. Do not leave anything blank. Turn the application in on time!

Step 2 Ask two teachers to write a letter of recommendation for you. Ask them to send it to the main office by October 5. The envelope should be sealed and labeled "Student Representative."

Step 3 Ask your parents to complete and sign a permission form. No one will be allowed to participate in the program without written permission. The form must be in the main office by October 5.

Step 4 You will be scheduled for an interview. Be on time! Dress neatly. Be prepared to tell the interviewer why you are the right person for the job. Bring a list of your skills and your strengths. Smile!

---

43. To apply for the position, students need help from   ELA6R1.e

    A. new students.

    B. town officials.

    C. parents and teachers.

    D. student representatives.

44. Which sentence **best** supports the topic sentence in paragraph 3?   ELA6R1.d

    A. Student reps decorate the bulletin board by the front door.

    B. Student reps write the *Spotlight* column in the local paper.

    C. All paperwork must be completed and turned in on time.

    D. The program meets on the first Tuesday of every month.

45. Why does the author
    underline part of the text?   ELA6RC2.f

    A. to show the text is important

    B. to show it is the heading of a list

    C. to show it is the start of a second
       article

    D. to show it is a quotation from the
       application

46. Why **most likely** did the   ELA6RC2.e
    author write the article?

    A. to increase the number of students
       attending the school

    B. to show the wide variety of pro-
       grams available to students

    C. to illustrate the one connection
       between the school and the town

    D. to explain the student rep position
       and application process to students

47. Step 4 of the article would   ELA6RC4.a
    also be helpful to

    A. students applying for an after-
       school job.

    B. teachers writing recommendation
       letters.

    C. students entering a new school.

    D. teachers meeting with parents.

48. What does the word   ELA6RC3.a
    process mean in the article?

    A. a legal action

    B. a series of steps

    C. movement in a straight line

    D. change made by manufacturing

49. What important   ELA6RC2.d
    information is missing
    from the article?

    A. where to find the applications

    B. when to turn in the application

    C. who benefits from the program

    D. how to submit recommendations

50. What sentence uses the   ELA6RC3.a
    word *outgoing* in the same
    way it is used in the article?

    A. Please place all of your outgoing
       mail in the wire basket.

    B. Two pipes are needed for the
       incoming and outgoing water.

    C. Her naturally friendly personality
       made her the most outgoing one in
       the group.

    D. The outgoing governor signed one
       last bill before the incoming gover-
       nor took office.

GA 6th Grade CRCT Reading
Practice Test 2

The purpose of this practice test is to measure your knowledge in reading comprehension. This practice test is based on the GPS-based CRCT standards for reading and adheres to the sample question format provided by the Georgia Department of Education.

General Directions:

1. Read all directions carefully.

2. Read each question or sample. Then choose the best answer.

3. Choose only one answer for each question. If you change an answer, be sure to erase your original answer completely.

Excerpt from *The Adventures of Reddy Fox*
by Thornton W. Burgess

(1) Every day Granny Fox led Reddy Fox over to the long railroad bridge and made him run back and forth across it until he had no fear of it whatever. At first it had made him dizzy, but now he could run across at the top of his speed and not mind it in the least. "I don't see what good it does to be able to run across a bridge; anyone can do that!" exclaimed Reddy one day.

(2) Granny Fox smiled. "Do you remember the first time you tried to do it?" she asked.

(3) Reddy hung his head. Of course he remembered—remembered that Granny had had to scare him into crossing that first time.

(4) Suddenly Granny Fox lifted her head. "Hark!" she exclaimed.

(5) Reddy pricked up his sharp, pointed ears. Way off back, in the direction from which they had come, they heard the baying of a dog. It wasn't the voice of Bowser the Hound but of a younger dog. Granny listened for a few minutes. The voice of the dog grew louder as it drew nearer.

(6) "He certainly is following our track," said Granny Fox. "Now, Reddy, you run across the bridge and watch from the top of the little hill over there. Perhaps I can show you a trick that will teach you why I have made you learn to run across the bridge."

(7) Reddy trotted across the long bridge and up to the top of the hill, as Granny had told him to. Then he sat down to watch. Granny trotted out in the middle of a field and sat down. Pretty soon a young hound broke out of the bushes, his nose in Granny's track. Then he looked up and saw her, and his voice grew still more savage and eager. Granny Fox started to run as soon as she was sure that the hound had seen her, but she did not run very fast. Reddy did not know what to make of it, for Granny seemed simply to be playing with the hound and not really trying to get away from him at all. Pretty soon Reddy heard another sound. It was a long, low rumble. Then there was a distant whistle. It was a train.

(8) Granny heard it, too. As she ran, she began to work back toward the long bridge. The train was in sight now. Suddenly Granny Fox started across the bridge so fast that she looked like a little red streak. The dog was close at her heels when she started and he was so eager to catch her that he didn't see either the bridge or the train. But he couldn't begin to run as fast as Granny Fox. Oh, my, no! When she had reached the other side, he wasn't halfway across, and right behind him, whistling for him to get out of the way, was the train.

(9) The hound gave one frightened yelp, and then he did the only thing he could do; he leaped down, down into the swift water below, and the last Reddy saw of him he was frantically trying to swim ashore.

(10) "Now you know why I wanted you to learn to cross a bridge; it's a very nice way of getting rid of dogs," said Granny Fox, as she climbed up beside Reddy.

1. The author uses sensory details in paragraph 7 to help readers   ELA6R1.a

    A. hear and feel the approaching train.

    B. understand why Granny ran slowly.

    C. identify a new character in the story.

    D. see the cause of Reddy's confusion.

2. What is the purpose of the dialogue in the story?   ELA6R1.b

    A. to describe the details of the setting

    B. to explain why they don't fear Bowser

    C. to describe the main conflict in the story

    D. to show Granny and Reddy's relationship

3. What is the theme of the story?   ELA6R1.d

    A. Run faster than your enemies.

    B. Never be afraid of a tall bridge.

    C. Preparation is your best defense.

    D. A dog and a fox can never be friends.

4. The main conflict in the story can **best** be described as   ELA6R1.e.ii

    A. character versus self.

    B. character versus nature.

    C. character versus society.

    D. character versus character.

5. Which relationship is **most** like the Reddy/Granny relationship?   ELA6R1.e

    A. owner/pet

    B. friend/friend

    C. customer/clerk

    D. student/teacher

6. The story is told through the point of view of   ELA6R1.f

    A. Reddy.

    B. Granny.

    C. the young hound.

    D. an unnamed narrator.

7. Which is an example of personification?   ELA6R1.h.ii

    A. Granny Fox speaking

    B. Granny Fox running

    C. the young hound yelping

    D. the young hound chasing

Travel

by Edna St. Vincent Millay

The railroad track is miles away,
    And the day is loud with voices speaking, **(2)**
Yet there isn't a train goes by all day
    But I hear its whistle shrieking. **(4)**

All night there isn't a train goes by,
    Though the night is still for sleep and dreaming, **(6)**
But I see its cinders red on the sky,
    And hear its engine steaming. **(8)**

My heart is warm with the friends I make,
    And better friends I'll not be knowing, **(10)**
Yet there isn't a train I wouldn't take,
    No matter where it's going. **(12)**

8. The yearning tone of the   ELA6R1.g
poem is **best** shown through
the use of

  A. rhythm.

  B. off-rhyme.

  C. repetition.

  D. punctuation.

9. Lines 11 and 12 of the poem   ELA6R1.h.ii
contain an example of

  A. simile.

  B. metaphor.

  C. hyperbole.

  D. personification.

10. The setting of this poem is   ELA6R1.e
most likely

  A. in a big city.

  B. in the country.

  C. at a train station.

  D. in the narrator's home.

11. What message is found in   ELA6R1.d
the poem?

  A. Train travel is noisy and dirty.

  B. It is best to be alone in your travels.

  C. New friends are better than old
friends.

  D. The journey is as important as the
destination.

Budget-Friendly Gatherings

Have you been longing to host a party? Have your plans been stalled by money issues? Here is a plan that will satisfy your need to party with your need to keep an eye on the budget. Keep it simple. Those three little words will make all of the difference.

There are only three things you need for the perfect party: friends, fun, and food. Let's look at each step in order of importance.

Friends – As host, remember the most important ingredient in any party is the people. When it comes to invitations, remember our three word rule—keep it simple! Homemade invitations work just as well as store bought invitations. Make sure all necessary information is included. If you prefer, a phone call works, too. Don't get distracted by chatting with your friends about other things. Write the information out like a script, and use it to make your calls.

For example:

> Join us for a hike up Smith Mountain followed by Mike's Mug & Muffin Party
>
> When: Saturday, October 20, 1:30 p.m. – 4:00 p.m.
>
> Where: Smith House
>
> Host: Mike Smith

Special Instructions: Wear sturdy, comfortable shoes. Dress for the weather. B.Y.O.M. (Bring Your Own Mug…for great homemade hot chocolate!)

Fun – Have you ever attended a party where the guests sat and stared at each other? Avoid a social disaster by planning some form of entertainment. Again, remember those three words—keep it simple. Entertainment can be free. In the case of Mike Smith's party, the entertainment was a hike in the mountains behind his house. Other free outside activities, like skating on a frozen pond or playing softball, work well too. If you are concerned about weather, take it indoors. An evening of board games or a jigsaw puzzle race can be done with things you already own. Whether your entertainment will take place inside or outside, plan ahead.

Food – Once again—keep it simple! This is the area where your party budget will be spent. Keep your budget in mind. Also consider the preparation and clean-up time. You don't want your party to leave you feeling like you never want to repeat that mistake. In Mike's case, he needed to make or purchase muffins and heat up some hot chocolate as well as have paper plates and napkins available. Clean-up was simple too. He just had to collect the trash, sweep the floor, and clean the hot chocolate pots. His guests brought their mugs home to clean. Like Mike, you should respect your budget and your time when you make your food plan.

So find something to celebrate! Host a budget-friendly party soon. Remember—keep it simple!

12. Which is the topic sentence of section 2?   ELA6R1.a

  A. Have you ever attended a party where the guests sat and stared at each other?

  B. Avoid a social disaster by planning some form of entertainment.

  C. Again, remember those three words—keep it simple.

  D. Whether your entertainment will take place inside or outside, plan ahead.

13. The author organized the information in the article in   ELA6R1.c

  A. time order.

  B. spatial order.

  C. order of importance.

  D. cause and effect order.

14. Which detail sentence would **best** support the main idea of section 1?   ELA6R1.d

  A. Parties aren't limited to special occasions.

  B. Everyone can become a great host or hostess.

  C. Keep the party space in mind when deciding how many guests to invite.

  D. Sometimes it is more fun to be a guest at a gathering your friend is hosting.

15. What step does the author recommend taking before making a phone invitation?   ELA6R1.e

  A. buy invitations

  B. write a script

  C. make invitations

  D. chat with your friends

16. Which is a message of the article?   ELA6RC.2

  A. It is easier to be a guest than a host.

  B. People are what make gatherings fun.

  C. A good guest cleans up after himself.

  D. Everyone should live on a tight budget.

17. Who would benefit **most** from this article?   ELA6RC2.d

  A. someone going to a party

  B. someone planning a party

  C. someone organizing a hiking club

  D. someone who owns an invitation shop

18. Why does the author repeat the phrase, "keep it simple?"   ELA6RC2.e

  A. to explain to guests why there are no decorations

  B. to encourage hosts to make everything themselves

  C. to persuade readers to consider time and budget when planning a party

  D. to explain why Mike had to ask his friends to bring something to the party

Hoops

(1) Dr. James Naismith could not have imagined how much the game would grow when he first invented the game of basketball. In 1891, Dr. Naismith worked in a school in Springfield, Massachusetts. The cold, snowy winters often stopped the children from playing outside. Dr. Naismith's goal was simple. He wanted to invent a game that school children could play indoors. He wanted to design a game that required skill over strength.

(2) Dr. Naismith started by writing thirteen rules for the game. Some of the rules, like the one that says players can't run with the ball, players still use today. Other rules have changed. Dr. Naismith's rules said that the only acceptable way of moving the ball down the court was by passing it among teammates. Today, players may dribble the ball. Although there are many more rules today than when Dr. Naismith designed the game, the goal of the game is basically the same—put the ball in the basket.

(3) Of course, the ball and the hoop have changed, too. Dr. Naismith nailed two wooden peach baskets to the wall. The players used a soccer ball to play. Their goal was to get the soccer ball into their team's basket. When they made a basket, someone climbed a ladder to retrieve the ball from the basket. Today, players toss a basketball through a metal hoop and net. The ball falls out of the open bottom of the net. The peach baskets are gone, but the term **making a basket** remains. More than 100 years later, players have the same goal as the players on the first team—making a basket.

	Then	**Now**
Players	9 per team on court	5 per team on court
Equipment	Soccer ball/peach baskets	Basketball, metal rim, net
Rules	13	100+
Goal	Ball in basket	Ball in basket

19. Which graphic feature in the article is used to compare and contrast the game of basketball over time? ELA6R1.b

    A. chart

    B. bold font

    C. illustration

    D. underlining

20. What information in the chart is not found in the article? ELA6RC2.f

    A. At first, players used a soccer ball to play basketball.

    B. At first, nine players on each team were on the court.

    C. Today the basketball hoop is made with a metal rim and a net.

    D. Today players can both dribble and pass the ball to each other.

21. What is the main idea of paragraph 3? ELA6R1.d

    A. Long ago, players used a soccer ball to play basketball.

    B. Today the basket is made of a metal rim and a bottomless net.

    C. Although the equipment has changed, the goal of the game has remained the same.

    D. The earliest basketball players needed two peach baskets and a ladder to play the game.

22. What was the author's purpose for writing this article? ELA6RC2.e

    A. to teach readers how to play basketball

    B. to entertain readers with a funny story

    C. to inform readers about the history of basketball

    D. to explain to readers how inventors get their ideas

Use the dictionary entry to answer the following question.

dribble *v.* 1. to flow in drips

2. to drool

3. to move with short bounces

4. to issue in small bits

23. Which entry **best** matches the way *dribble* is used in paragraph 2? ELA6R3.a

    A. entry 1

    B. entry 2

    C. entry 3

    D. entry 4

Barton's Butterfly Center

Save the Butterflies!

Butterflies might begin to disappear off the earth, if we don't do our part to save them. Widespread construction is destroying many butterfly habitats. Mother Nature needs our help. You can help conserve these beautiful and necessary insects. If you don't want to see the balance of nature lost, plant a butterfly garden.

A butterfly garden consists of two main parts. The first part is host plants, like clover and sassafras. While in the caterpillar stage of life, your insect guests eat the host plants. The second main part is food plants, such as the Butterfly Bush and Rose of Sharon. The butterflies dine on the nectar of the food plants. To encourage butterfly visits, you must provide both.

Barton's Butterfly Center shares in your concern for these beautiful creatures. We are here to help you help them. We produce the finest host and food plants in the majestic state of Georgia. Our experts can help you plan the perfect setting for butterflies to call home. With our help, your garden could become the most popular spot for butterflies in your area! Stop by today to learn more about how you can help save the butterfly population.

They need our help. Together we can do it.

Barton's Butterfly Houses

Nothing says welcome like a Barton Butterfly House. Our houses provide a warm place for butterflies on chilly nights. They invite butterflies in and keep birds and squirrels out. The houses also look great in your yard. They make every garden more beautiful.

Last spring, I planted a butterfly garden in my side yard. My wife and I enjoyed many afternoons sitting on our porch, watching the butterflies. This would not have been possible without Barton's Butterfly Center.

Jake Johnson, professional landscaper

Read this sentence from the Web page.

Butterflies might begin to disappear off the earth, if we don't do our part to save them.

24. The sentence is an example of the propaganda technique known as ELA6LSV2.a

   A. testimonial.

   B. bandwagon.

   C. hidden fears.

   D. unfinished comparisons.

25. The author's use of the words *destroying* and *conserve* is an example of the technique known as ELA6LSV2.a

   A. hidden fears.

   B. loaded words.

   C. glittering generality.

   D. card stacking.

26. Which paragraph is an
example of the
testimonial technique?

ELA6LSV2.a

A. second paragraph

B. third paragraph

C. box about houses

D. letter from landscaper

27. The last sentence in
paragraph 1 is an example
of the technique known as

ELA6LSV2.a

A. repetition.

B. bandwagon.

C. hidden fears.

D. name calling.

28. Which sentence in
paragraph 3 is an example
of "plain folks appeal"?

ELA6LSV2.a

A. Barton's Butterfly Center shares in
your concern for these beautiful
creatures.

B. We produce the finest host and
food plants in the majestic state of
Georgia.

C. Our experts can help you plan the
perfect setting for butterflies to call
home.

D. Stop by today to learn more about
how you can help save the butterfly
population.

29. What was the author's
purpose for writing this
Web site?

ELA6RC2.e

A. to explain how to grow a butterfly
garden

B. to persuade people to buy butterfly
plants

C. to inform people about a problem
in nature

D. to describe the benefits of butterfly
gardens

30. What is the meaning of
host as it is used in
paragraph 2?

ELA6RC3.a

A. a very large number

B. one who entertains socially

C. a living thing that supports another
living thing

D. a rock that is older than the miner-
als found in it

Piero's Desire

(1) Piero slipped away from the crowd and hurried down the narrow alley. The doors and windows all looked alike to him here. Determined to get a glimpse of the man, Piero vowed to peek through every dusty window, every open door. His father had scoffed when Piero told him of his desire. "Leonardo da Vinci is not famous," he had said. "He has not accomplished anything of importance. Look around you. Our city is full of artists, writers, and musicians; talk to them. They have more to say than Leonardo does."

(2) Piero wanted to be an obedient son, but he had heard the whispers. He had heard the people in the streets utter Leonardo's name in hushed voices. They called him a great artist, writer, and inventor. Piero wanted to see this genius work; he wanted to hear him speak. He hoped it would help him envision the world through the eyes of his unknown hero.

(3) He continued on his journey from building to building, his heels clattering against the pavement. Disappointment greeted him at every stop. Piero had almost abandoned hope by the time he reached the final building. He polished the window glass with his sleeve, pressed his forehead against the pane, and peered inside. Piero's heart pounded against his chest; perhaps, he had found his prize. In the center of a room, a man sat bent over a table. His beard scraped the wooden surface; his right hand rested awkwardly beside a drawing. Piero looked from paper to paper, and then back to the man. A sudden gust of air pushed through the alley, causing Piero to shiver. The wind whistled a warning: "Do not disturb."

---

31. As it is used in paragraph 1, the word *scoffed* means   `ELA6R2.a`

    A. "investigated a motive."

    B. "reflected one's opinion."

    C. "made something seem worthless."

    D. "took time to consider thoroughly."

32. The root word *vis* means to see. What does the word *envision* mean as it is used in paragraph 2?   `ELA6R2.b`

    A. to picture in your own mind

    B. to become a famous inventor

    C. to be respectful to your parent

    D. to understand someone's ideas

33. In paragraph 3, the word *clattering* is an example of   `ELA6R1.h.ii`

    A. simile.

    B. metaphor.

    C. hyperbole.

    D. onomatopoeia.

34. The story **most closely** reflects events that occurred during which historical period?   `ELA6R1.c`

    A. the Classical Age

    B. the Age of Reform

    C. the Italian Renaissance

    D. the Industrial Revolution

35. Which sentence from the story is an example of inner conflict?   ELA6R1.e.i

    A. His father had scoffed when Piero told him of his desire.

    B. Piero wanted to be an obedient son, but he had heard the whispers.

    C. In the center of a room, a man sat bent over a table.

    D. A sudden gust of air pushed through the alley, causing Piero to shiver.

36. Which sentence contains an example of personification?   ELA6R1.a

    A. The doors and windows all looked alike to him here.

    B. Our city is full of artists, writers, and musicians; talk to them.

    C. Disappointment greeted him at every stop.

    D. Piero looked from paper to paper, and then back to the man.

37. What is the purpose of the dialogue in the story?   ELA6R1.b

    A. to establish the time period

    B. to establish the writer's point of view

    C. to explain how Piero knows about Leonardo

    D. to explain why Piero wants to meet Leonardo

What Are the Odds of That?

You race home from the store with a new board game under your arm and three of your friends by your side. You gather around the kitchen table, each choose one of the dice, and begin to play. Each of the first three players rolls a "4" on his die and moves his playing piece ahead four spaces to the Billionaire Bonus square. Now, it's your turn. You study the die in your hand. It has six sides. Each side has a different numeral on it. What are the odds that you will roll a "4" too? There is one "4" on the die and six possible outcomes. Therefore, the probability that you will roll a "4" is 1 in 6, the exact same odds each of your friends had. You roll the die, but are disappointed to see it land with the "6" face up. There will be no Billionaire Bonus for you.

What went wrong? Nothing—at least not mathematically speaking. It's true you had a 1 in 6 chance of rolling a "4" but you also had a 5 in 6 chance of not rolling a "4." Unfortunately, for your bank account, the odds were against you. The probability of an event occurring is equal to the number of ways an event can happen (there is only one "4" on the dice), divided by the number of possible outcomes (there are six sides, each a different numeral, so there are six possible outcomes).

Try a little experiment with your die. Select a new number. Roll the die twelve times in a row keeping a tally of how often your number lands face up. Did you roll your numeral twice? It's possible, but the laws of probability are not on your side. Each roll of the die is a separate event in the experiment, so each event has the same probability—1 in 6. The outcome of one event does not influence the outcome of the next event. The formula stays the same no matter how many times you roll the dice.

A Mathematical Formula

Number of Ways an Event Can Occur ÷ Number of Possible Outcomes = Probability of Event

Glossary

Event: one trial of an experiment

Odds: the degree of likeliness of something happening

Outcome: the result of a single trial of an experiment

Probability: the measure of how likely an event is

	1	2	3	4	5	6
Number of Ways an Event Can Occur	1	1	1	1	1	1
Number of Possible Outcomes	6	6	6	6	6	6

38. According to the glossary, which two words mean the same thing?   ELA6R1.a

    A. event and odds

    B. odds and outcome

    C. odds and probability

    D. outcome and probability

39. According to the chart, which statement is correct?   ELA6R1.b

    A. The probability of rolling a "3" face-up on a die is three in six.

    B. There are thirty-six possible outcomes each time you roll a die.

    C. Each numeral has an equal probability of landing face up on any given roll.

    D. If you roll a single die six times, the numeral 6 will land face up one time.

40. What is the main idea of the final paragraph?   ELA6R1.d

    A. Each roll of the die is a separate event.

    B. An experiment includes twelve rolls of the die.

    C. You cannot determine the probability of a number landing face up.

    D. If you roll the die twelve times, your numeral might land face up twice.

41. Who would **most** benefit from the article?   ELA6RC2.d

    A. a math student

    B. a math teacher

    C. a game designer

    D. a store clerk

42. What was the author's purpose for writing the article?   ELA6RC2.e

    A. to describe a new game

    B. to persuade you to buy a game

    C. to explain mathematical probability

    D. to model how to conduct an experiment

43. In which sentence does the word *roll* have the same meaning as in the underlined sentence in the first paragraph?   ELA6R2.c

    A. I made you a sandwich on a fresh roll.

    B. I bought a roll of paper towels at the store.

    C. Listen carefully as the teacher takes roll call.

    D. Can you roll the ball to the next person in line?

44. The meaning of *formula* in the last sentence of the article can **best** be determined by   ELA6RC4.c

    A. skimming the chart.

    B. skimming the glossary.

    C. rereading the last sentence.

    D. rereading the last paragraph.

The Last Night of Summer

(1) "Look at that one, Emily," Gran said. "That's a good luck elephant."

(2) I studied the cloud that hung above us and listened as Gran pointed out the trunk, tail, and feet in the fluffy animal cloud. Her voice was like an old woolen blanket, rough and scratchy, yet warm and soothing. The air, sensing our need for a new scene, gently pushed the elephant away in search of other animal clouds. The effect was that of a velvet curtain sweeping open, unveiling a hidden stage.

(3) Gran's sigh exposed her deep contentment. I propped myself up on my elbows and looked over at her. She was stretched out on her back, her head resting on a pillow made of her neatly folded jacket. Her eyes shone like the stars she was gazing at. "Let's play connect the stars," Gran suggested.

(4) I settled back down onto the ground and began drawing cars, candlesticks, and camels with the stars. When I finished an elaborate construction of the Statue of Liberty, Gran chuckled. "I'll give you an A+ for creative thinking, but those last three dots aren't really stars."

(5) Before I could protest, my "stars" flickered and the fireflies that had formed Lady Liberty's torch flew away. I wanted to somehow capture the creatures, to demand that they stay suspended over us. I wanted this moment, this feeling to last forever. As if she could read my mind, Gran said, "I will remember this evening forever."

---

45. The author uses dialogue in the story to   ELA6R1.b

   A. show conflict.

   B. describe the setting.

   C. explain why Emily is there.

   D. show what Gran is thinking.

46. Which point of view is used to tell the story?   ELA6R1.f

   A. first person, Gran

   B. third person, Gran

   C. first person, Emily

   D. third person, Emily

47. What word **best** describes the tone of the story?   ELA6R1.g

   A. angry

   B. peaceful

   C. mysterious

   D. melancholy

48. Which plot summary of   ELA6RC4.a
another story is most like
the plot of "The Last Night of
Summer"?

   A. A father and son walk through the
woods noticing the animals who
live there.

   B. A teacher grades a student based
on the student's efforts instead of
on the results.

   C. Two old friends experience the
excitement of opening night at an
outdoor theater.

   D. A family's late summer picnic is
ruined by the invasion of an army
of hungry ants.

49. Which sentence uses the   ELA6RC3.a
word *suspended* in the
same way it is used in paragraph 5?

   A. The principal suspended the
students from school for three
days.

   B. Some of the train routes were suspended because of the snowstorm.

   C. The decorations were suspended
from the ceiling by invisible wires.

   D. She never suspended service to the
families who could not pay on
time.

Read the sentence from the story.

Her voice was like an old woolen blanket,
rough and scratchy, yet warm and soothing.

The sentence contains an   ELA6R1.a
example of

50.

   A. simile.

   B. metaphor.

   C. hyperbole.

   D. personification.

A

action
    falling 103, 105
    rising 103, 105
affix (word) 146
alliteration 88, 90, 131
antagonist 99, 105
antonym 144, 150
association 56
author
    attitude 120
    purpose 20, 22
    purpose, types of 19, 25
    tone 120

B

bandwagon technique 54

C

caption 66, 73
card stacking 54
cause 44
character
    types of 99
characterization 105
chart 70, 73
claim
    support 22
climax 103, 105
conflict 102
    types of 100
context clue 141, 142, 144, 150

D

definition 45
description 114, 123
detail
    supporting 32, 33
diagram 68, 73
dialogue 111, 123
dictionary, 64

E

effect 44

F

figurative language 79
    types of 80, 82, 83, 85, 86, 88, 89, 90

G

glittering generalities 55
glossary 63, 64, 73
graph 73
    types of 68
graphic
    organizer 65, 66
    types of 65, 66, 68
    types of (in poetry) 135
graphic (in poetry 137

H

homograph 145
hyperbole 85, 90

I

idea
    main 32
    main, hidden 34
    supporting 32, 33
idiom 80, 90
illustration 66, 68, 73
index 63, 64, 73
informational text 53

L

language
    figurative 79
literary
    element, types of 100
literature
    types of 21, 22, 25

M

message 119, 123
metaphor 82, 83, 90

N

narrator 123
    signal words 117

O

onomatopoeia 89, 90, 133, 137
order
    cause and effect 44, 48
    classification 45, 48
    comparison and contrast 45, 48
    definition 45
    logical 41, 45, 48
    sequence of events 41, 48
    time 41
organization
    graphic 73
    tools 41
    types of 41, 44, 45, 48
organizer
    graphic 63

P

paragraph
    parts of 32, 37
person
    first 117

third 117
personification 86
plot 105
    parts of 102
poetry 129
point of view 117, 123
prefix 146
propaganda 53
    types of 54, 55, 56
prose 129
protagonist 99, 105

R

repetition 56
resolution 103, 105
rhyme scheme 134, 137
root (word) 146

S

sensory detail 79
sentence
    concluding 32, 33
    topic 32, 35
setting 105
    historical 115, 123
simile 83, 90
sound
    device (in poetry) 131
    device, types of 131, 133
    pattern (in poetry) 131
sound device
    types of 137
story
    characterization 97
    element, types of 111, 114
    narrator 117
    setting 95
    structure 95, 97
suffix 146
synonym 144, 150

T

table 70, 71
testimonial 55
text
    evaluate 70, 71
    evaluating 73
    features 70
    informational 34, 70
    informational, types of 63
theme 123
    implied 119
    stated directly 119
tip
    finding main idea 35
    for finding main idea 37
tone (in poetry and prose) 129, 130
transfer propaganda technique 56
transition 41, 44, 46, 48

V

Venn Diagram 66
vocabulary
    skill 141, 150
    strategy 141, 144

W

word meaning 144
    affix 146
    multiple 145
    prefix 146
    root 146
    suffix 146
    multiple 150